C000049691

cover to cover

Bible Companion

Bible Companion

Easy to Use Reference
to Understanding the Bible

CWR, Waverley Abbey House, Waverley Lane, Farnham, Surrey GU9 8EP

UK: (and countries not listed below)
CWR, PO Box 230, Farnham, Surrey GU9 8XG.
Tel: (01252) 784710 Outside UK (44) 1252 784710

AUSTRALIA: CMC Australasia, PO Box 519, Belmont, Victoria 3216. Tel: (03) 5241 3288

CANADA: CMC Distribution Ltd, PO Box 7000, Niagara on the Lake, Ontario L0S 1J0.
Tel: (0800) 325 1297

GHANA: Challenge Enterprises of Ghana, PO Box 5723, Accra.
Tel: (021) 222437/223249 Fax: (021) 226227

HONG KONG: Cross Communications Ltd, 1/F, 562A Nathan Road, Kowloon.
Tel: 2780 1188 Fax: 2770 6229

INDIA: Crystal Communications, 10-3-18/4/1, East Marredpally, Secunderabad – 500 026.
Tel/Fax: (040) 7732801

KENYA: Keswick Bookshop, PO Box 10242, Nairobi. Tel: (02) 331692/226047

MALAYSIA: Salvation Book Centre (M) Sdn Bhd, 23 Jalan SS 2/64, 47300 Petaling Jaya, Selangor.
Tel: (03) 78766411/78766797 Fax: (03) 78757066/78756360

NEW ZEALAND: CMC New Zealand Ltd, Private Bag, 17910 Green Lane, Auckland.
Tel: (09) 5249393 Fax: (09) 5222137

NIGERIA: FBFM, Helen Baugh House, 96 St Finbarr's College Road, Akoka, Lagos.
Tel: (01) 7747429/4700218/825775/827264

PHILIPPINES: OMF Literature Inc, 776 Boni Avenue, Mandaluyong City.
Tel: (02) 531 2183 Fax: (02) 531 1960

REPUBLIC OF IRELAND: Scripture Union, 40 Talbot Street, Dublin 1.
Tel: (01) 8363764

SINGAPORE: Campus Crusade Asia Ltd, 315 Outram Road, 06-08 Tan Boon Liat Building,
Singapore 169074. Tel: (065) 222 3640

SOUTH AFRICA: Struik Christian Books, 80 MacKenzie Street, PO Box 1144, Cape Town 8000.
Tel: (021) 462 4360 Fax: (021) 461 3612

SRI LANKA: Christombu Books, 27 Hospital Street, Colombo 1.
Tel: (01) 433142/328909

TANZANIA: CLC Christian Book Centre, PO Box 1384, Mkwepu Street, Dar es Salaam.
Tel: (051) 2119439

UGANDA: New Day Bookshop, PO Box 2021, Kampala. Tel: (041) 255377

ZIMBABWE: Word of Life Books, Shop 4, Memorial Building, 35 S Machel Avenue, Harare.
Tel: (04) 781305 Fax: (04) 774739

For e-mail addresses, visit the CWR web site: **www.cwr.org.uk**

Cover to Cover Bible Companion
© CWR 2001

Concept development, editing, design and production by CWR
Cover photograph: Roger Walker
Diagrams: The Happy House
Internal Photographs: Roger Walker; PhotoDisc
Printed by: W S Bookwell
ISBN: 1 85345 172 X

Contents

Dear Friend,

The *Cover to Cover* series was born out of a vision to see more and more Christians deepen their relationship with God by reading His Word. So how wonderful it was to see more than half a million people join the *Cover to Cover* community in its first year alone; a group that continues to expand as we add new titles into the programme.

Many of you have asked for extra material that would place some of the key characters and events in context. We sought to meet that need with the *Cover to Cover* Website, which contains features and commentary as well as a lively online discussion forum. Much of this material is now available to you in this one helpful reference.

I hope and pray that through these simple studies you will draw closer to God. Every minute you spend searching for clearer understanding of His Word is the best life investment you will ever make.

God Bless You

Selwyn Hughes

(Co-author of *Cover to Cover* and *God's People*)

Key Contributors

Philip Greenslade

Philip Greenslade is an internationally respected writer, theologian and teacher. He has been a Theological Consultant and has taught at the Elim Bible College (now Regent College) in England. Philip came to CWR in 1991, developing and teaching some of our most successful programmes and as part of the ministry team he has taken seminars to many parts of the world. A popular speaker, he often presents *Cover to Cover Bible Discovery* weekends on a range of fascinating subjects and he is the major contributor to *God's Story*, the third title in the *Cover to Cover* series, published in 2002.

Trevor J. Partridge

Trevor Partridge holds a degree in theology. He has travelled extensively teaching and preaching in seminars, conferences and churches around the world and is a popular author and Bible teacher. For 24 years he was involved in the ministry of CWR, developing Waverley Abbey House and its training programmes, serving as Executive Director and making a regular contribution to the *Every Day with Jesus* Further Study section. He is founder and director of New Horizon Ministries, a fresh initiative in pastoral care.

Ian Sewter

Ian Sewter first became involved with CWR in 1978 when he began writing for *Young People's Every Day with Jesus*. Ian has also compiled a number of Further Study sections for *Every Day with Jesus*, written for our *Revival* magazine and has been a major contributor to the *Cover to Cover* Website. Ian is a member of the leadership team of his local church and his passion is that the written Word should become a living Word in people's hearts bringing them to maturity in Christ.

Forum Voice

The Forum Voice entries in this book are only made possible thanks to the dynamic, challenging and fascinating contributions made to the *Cover to Cover* discussion forum. Readers from across the globe met at the Website to share their comments, queries, questions and thoughts. The best of the "conversations" have been edited for this Companion, and we would like to take this opportunity to thank everyone who made the forum such a success. You can join in current conversations today at www.cover2cover.org

A Guide to the Companion

This *Cover to Cover Bible Companion* is arranged in 12 sections, which follow the chronological pattern of the first *Cover to Cover* title. Each section will contain some, or all of the following features:

Insight

In these in-depth articles Philip Greenslade brings his unique approach and thoughtful observations to explore some key theological and spiritual implications around the main biblical events.

Bible Lives

Ian Sewter provides a window into the lives of a number of the Bible characters featured in *God's People*; helping us to understand our own experiences and learn valuable lessons.

In Detail

Helpful articles inspired by the comments on the Forum. Ian Sewter reveals how the Truth of Scripture can be found in the tiniest detail.

Forum Voice

The *Cover to Cover* online forum has produced lively discussions and informed comments and challenging questions. The best of these contributions have been edited for the Companion. The views expressed by *Cover to Cover* readers do not necessarily represent those of CWR as an organisation. Ian Sewter provides the "*Cover to Cover* Responds" feedback.

On Reflection

The *Discussion Starters* have been a popular feature on the Website, and here you can read some of the more personal and reflective extracts to help you apply God's Word into your own experience.

Please Note:
You will also find a helpful and easy-to-use index at the back of the book where you can search by name, place, book or term.

Why Read the Bible at All?

The Bible, in its various translations, remains the best selling title in the world. Yet some studies have suggested that Bible reading is at an all time low. So, what can we expect to gain from studying Scripture? What will we learn in our attempt to explore The Word? Why read the Bible at all?

Insight

The answer is because as you read the Bible you discover God's story. Jesus proved with His parables that there's no better way to communicate God than through stories, and this is what the Bible essentially is – a thrilling, action-packed adventure with God, one in which we can play a part. It is not a pick-and-mix catalogue of religious goodies or spiritual recipes. It is not an occult code to be deciphered by elite disciples. And the Bible most definitely is not a compendium of texts which we can use to buttress our own theological position.

Under pressure to "make the Bible relevant", too often we trivialize or water down its overall message, reducing its impact to slogans and soundbites. We can end up draining the Bible of its colour. We squeeze the life out of it and render it a "flat" book, a bland moral mandate with passionless principles. But this is not the way the Bible came to us. It came as a story – a vast, sprawling, untidy, story, but a story nonetheless. It's not always the easiest book to read, but it is the most rewarding and enriching.

As rambling, muddled and topsy-turvy as this long histori-cal story can be, we can nonetheless find God at its centre, because He's the author. In saying that God has authored this story we are recognising that the threads of meaning, and the trajectories of truth are all part of His sovereign plan. It is the One Creator God who initiates

Insight

this story. And as this One Creator God supervises His creation, steering it in the face of history's setbacks and rebuffs, we find out who this God really is!

It's in the gripping narrative, showing us how God achieves His purpose, that we discover what kind of God this God is. God is not only the author of the story but He is the chief actor in it too. He works from the inside not the outside. So God shouldn't be seen as an "Olympian" figure, detached from the achievements and struggles of His creation. Rather He has chosen to fully immerse Himself in the story, making Himself vulnerable to its pain and ambiguity.

By working within – not outside – the drama, God leaves Himself exposed to misunderstanding, He puts His reputation for holiness and omnipotence on the line and risks His good name through association with some pretty shady characters. In short, God is willing to become the God of Abraham, Isaac, and even Jacob!

God is not only the author of the story but also the chief actor in it too.

Meeting God like this in His own story we find a God who is involved, intimate, wild, passionate, unpredictable, utterly faithful, vulnerable, open, persuadable – a tough and tender God who travels and travails with Israel, a God with genuine emotions.

God never thought that being God was something to be exploited to His own selfish advantage, but humbled Himself to the level of His human partners, submitting to bear the cost of whatever His creation might come to! Which brings us to Jesus.

This is why we really need to read the Bible – because it leads us to Christ. As they live in and through the biblical story the attentive Bible reader soon begins to experience the story's cumulative effect. Jesus gathers in all the historical threads that weave through the Old Testament and makes sense of them all. The story of Christ is the climax of the earlier parts of God's story and the key to its unfolding in the future. Without the Old Testament we cannot begin to understand Jesus, and without Jesus the Old Testament makes no final sense.

We read the Bible because it tells our story too.

When we search the Scriptures looking to find eternal life, we will inevitably come to Jesus to whom all the Scriptures point. Luke 24:32: "Did not our hearts burn within us as he opened the Scriptures to us on the road" marvelled the Emmaus Two. From Moses through the prophets, He explained to them how the long redemptive story of God was filled-full by His life and His death and His resurrection. In Jesus all the promise-plans of God converge. The Israel story is conclusively redrawn, the world's story is redeemed and rewritten and the story of God is fully revealed to us.

We read the Bible because it tells our story too. "The Bible seeks to catch us up in a grand narrative, a great saga of God's dealings with humanity – a saga begun in God's journey with Israel, continued in the surprising call of God even unto gentiles. The church is the product of that story", wrote William Willimon.

As we immerse ourselves in this big biblical story we encounter the real God, and get to find out what He's

Insight

really like! As we re-live God's story with Him we find ourselves saved and shaped by it. We learn to appreciate the satisfying unity of Scripture while enjoying its fascinating diversity, constantly getting drawn into its action, finding ourselves caught up in the saving movement of God.

By reading the Bible we learn to "indwell" the story more and more, so looking out on our contemporary world through more biblical eyes. We stop trying to make the Bible relevant to our modern lives and begin to find instead that we are being made increasingly relevant to the Bible.

> ## As we re-live God's story with Him we find ourselves saved and shaped by it.

Professor Gary Burge of Wheaton College recently lamented the inability of many of his evangelical students to put major events and characters of the Bible in the correct linear order. They just didn't know what comes where in God's great story. "No one", he says, "is announcing that the biblical story is The Story that defines our identity and life in the church." Well, some of us are trying to do just that. In studying the Bible with the *Cover to Cover* series you are on a passage to defining yourself within the context of God's story. Enjoy your journey of discovery. Then enjoy it again.

Adam

It is suggested that Adam was named after the dust of the ground from which he was formed, as illustrated in Genesis 2:7. This thought is continued in Genesis 3:19, which reveals that we were made of dust and when we die it is to dust we will return. In a sense, we are no different to the grass of the field which springs up, flourishes but for a moment and then withers and falls (Isa. 40:6–8).

Yet there is something preciously different about humankind because when God formed Adam He breathed life into him in a way that life was not given to the rest of creation. In fact the literal translation of Genesis 2:7 is that God breathed the breath of lives into man. Adam did not just have a physical life but he also possessed a soul and a spirit life that could commune with God who is Spirit (John 4:24).

It appears from Genesis 3:8 that God would regularly walk with Adam in the Garden during the evening when they would fellowship and talk together. Scientists have calculated the worth of the human body as only a few pounds in currency for we are only made of common elements of the earth, but in reality the body is only an outer shell to house our priceless inner life of soul and spirit. Our soul gives us personality with emotions and thoughts, but it is our spirit that primarily enables us to contact and commune with our Creator.

When Adam sinned it was his spirit that was deadened

BibleLives

and it is that dead spirit that has been passed on to the rest of the human race like a faulty gene. That is why Jesus said that we needed a spiritual birth in addition to our physical birth (John 3:3–8). Just as the first Adam was the progenitor of the sinful human race, Jesus, the second Adam, is the One who gives life to a new people of righteousness (Rom. 5:12–21).

The hymnist wrote, "Breathe on me breath of God, fill me with life anew." Indeed, we have received the treasure of the Holy Spirit into our physical bodies just as a clay jar might contain gold and precious jewels (2 Cor. 4:7). As we study God's people in Scripture we need to learn to avoid repeating their mistakes, but seek to emulate their faith and become the very people God originally designed us to be.

Adam was chosen by God to be His image-bearer and represent Him on earth. Where he failed, we have been chosen as a part of the Church of Jesus Christ to be ambassadors to work for God's kingdom to come on earth as it is in heaven. Above all, we are not just dust of the ground because we have been born again by the precious Word of God and given eternal life such that when our physical body dies it is actually a release of our spirit into Paradise with Christ.

For Further Study

1 Pet. 1:23–25
1 Cor. 15:20–58
2 Cor. 5:1–8

Noah

Noah is one of the Old Testament characters specifically listed in Hebrews 11 as an example of a person of faith. It is said in Hebrews 11:7 that he responded to God in an act of obedience with an attitude of holy fear and in so doing became a pattern for us to follow.

One of the most difficult issues we face in our lives is the courage to be different and not conform to the crowd. Genesis 6:11–12 records how the people on earth at that time were totally corrupt, violent and their thoughts were only of evil, not of good. Noah stood out as a shining beacon through his lifestyle as the one exception of righteousness and refused to join in with the wickedness of those around him.

God chose Noah to be the saviour of a world that was destined for judgment and through his work and witness a remnant were saved to re-populate a new earth. He was, according to 2 Peter 2:5, a preacher of righteousness. In this respect he is such a great example to us, for our responsibility is to preach the gospel of salvation regardless of how many people actually believe and join the Church. Our holy lifestyle and fearless witness is to be a light in the darkness to those around us (Matt. 5:14–16; Eph. 5:8).

Noah is also a "type" of Christ. In other words, his life story in some way reflects the life and ministry of Jesus. Noah prepared a way to escape the impending judgment of God for those who would believe and follow him. The

ark itself was coated with pitch as a protective covering (Gen. 6:14). The Hebrew word for pitch is *kaphar* and is translated elsewhere in the Old Testament as atonement and usually refers to the process where a sinful person is reconciled to God and protected or saved from judgment.

In the New Testament it is because of Jesus Christ, our ark of protection and atonement (1 Pet. 3:20–21), that we receive reconciliation with God (Rom. 5:11) and are saved from judgment (John 3:36).

The story of Noah's drunkenness only serves to prove that God is not looking for perfect people, but for those who, despite their human imperfections, have set their hearts to follow and obey Him to the best of their abilities.

Job

Job is a book which is as relevant today as it was 4000 years ago. Much of (Western) Christianity seems to be obsessed with God's blessings of wealth, health and happiness. The story of Job reminds us in no uncertain terms that believers lives may involve pain, persecution and even loss of possessions!

The very name, Job, means "persecuted", "hated" or "enemy". Many Christians throughout the world are suffering persecution because of their faith just like Job. The same enemy who attacked Job, Satan, seeks to attack us and destroy our faith. This is why the New Testament uses Job's life as an example to us in James 5:10–11; "Take the old prophets as your mentors. They put up with anything, went through everything, and never once quit, all the time honouring God. What a gift life is to those who stay the course! You've heard, of course, of Job's staying power, and you know how God brought it all together for him at the end. That's because God cares, cares right down to the last detail." (*The Message* paraphrase)

The phrase that is often used about the "patience of Job" is more correctly translated as "endurance" or "perseverance". We may wait patiently for hours for a train, but that involves no real pain, suffering or crisis of faith. Endurance is totally different. It involves a refusal to give up in the face of great opposition or overwhelming grief.

A mother could wait patiently for her lost children to

return home during a raging storm or she could go out and endure the tempest to find them. Many Bible characters persevered through apparently impossible situations and refused to deny their faith even when faced with death. The three Hebrews faced with torture and execution by fire declared, "If we are thrown into the flaming furnace, our God is able to deliver us ... But if he doesn't, please understand, sir, that even then we will never under any circumstance serve your gods or worship the golden statue you have erected." (Dan. 3:17–18 TLB).

In the face of loss we are sometimes all too ready, as Job's wife advised, to "curse God and die" (Job. 2:9). Consider for a moment the losses that Job suffered. He lost his possessions, he lost his children, he lost his health, he lost compassionate friends ("you must have sinned"), and he temporarily lost the certainty of his faith ("why do you oppress me while you smile on the schemes of the wicked?"). Yet through it all Job did not curse God or cease to believe in Him.

Job's responses have become classic sayings in many languages; "Naked I came from my mother's womb, and naked I shall depart", "The Lord gave and the Lord has taken away; may the name of the Lord be praised" and "Though He slay me, yet will I hope in him". We recognise of course that Job did express his emotions and honest questions to God, but at no time did he renege on his faith. In fact, Job later acknowledged that his trials even served to deepen his relationship with God (Job 42:1–5).

Like Job, our own trials of faith can work to strengthen our spiritual life and experience the comfort of the Holy Spirit (Rom. 5:3–5, 8:28; Jam. 1:2–4; 1 Pet. 1:6–7). Paradise is only found in heaven where "there will be no more death, nor sorrow, nor crying, nor pain". Until then, our lives on this earth will inevitably be affected by accident, sickness, poverty, broken relationships and death.

For the Christian there may also be the added suffering of persecution, temptation, satanic attack and trials of faith. This is not meant to be negative, only a realistic assessment of the consequences of living in a fallen world. Yet in all these things we are persuaded that nothing can separate us from the love of God in Jesus Christ. We can, like Job, patiently endure with God's strength and echo the cry of Habakkuk "though the fig-tree does not bud and there are no grapes on the vines, though the olive crop fails and the fields produce no food, though there are no sheep in the pen and no cattle in the stalls, yet I will rejoice in the Lord, I will be joyful in God my Saviour". Why can we rejoice like this in the face of adversity? Because, like Job, we know that, "God cares, cares right down to the last detail".

Creation and the Trinity

ForumVoice

FORUM VOICE
In my NIV it says "Let us make man in our image, in our likeness" Genesis 1:26, and I was wondering who does the "our" refer to?

FORUM VOICE
The "our" is referring to the trinity of Father, Son and Holy Spirit. In John 1 verse 1, this is talking about Jesus being with God at the beginning. Then in Genesis 1 verse 2, it speaks of the Spirit of God brooding over the waters. So at the beginning, you have three people quoted on the scene before any creating. This is one of the amazing mysteries of our God.

FORUM VOICE
I puzzled over the trinity for some while. A well respected teacher in the church where I grew up suggested than synergy – where the sum of the whole is greater than the individual parts – was a way of considering the problem. He posed the question: What does 1x1x1 equal?

Temptation in the Garden

FORUM VOICE
Why did God leave Satan in the Garden of Eden? Bearing in mind that God is omnipotent, omniscient and omnipresent, all seeing, all knowing and present everywhere; why did He put the Tree of Knowledge in the Garden? He must have already known that the snake would tempt Eve and Eve, Adam?

FORUM VOICE
God created people to have a relationship with Him, but a relationship which wasn't forced or shackled in any way. If we have to obey it's not freedom, it's a dictatorship. The long or the short of it is that people did rebel against God, breaking that relationship – and that required another tree – the tree of calvary.

FORUM VOICE
Do you not think that the account of the Garden of Eden gives us a heart rendering view of what it is like to be in the presence of God, and away from God's presence? One of the things that God requires from His people is obedience. It seems to me that it all comes down to faith. Eve was tempted because she displayed a lack of obedience, she failed to appreciate fully what God had given. Trust had been broken, and the relationship flawed. This always happens when we think we know best.

FORUM VOICE
Why did God leave Satan in the Garden? Well if there is no Satan, then there is no choice to do evil. You can't do anything but be good – and that is no choice at all. God so values our ability to choose, that He gives us free choice, even if that means sending his Son to bail us out. Give it a minute's thought. That's amazing. God is sovereign. God does know the future, and He could see that Adam was going to sin, but the fact that God could see into the future had no effect on Adam's choice.

Forum Voice

COVER TO COVER RESPONDS

When reading the Bible we need to be careful that we do not read between the lines and see something that is not there. For example, the Bible does not say that the serpent was left in the Garden, it only focuses on the expulsion of Adam and Eve. In Genesis we are not told what actually happened to the serpent. It is so frustrating of God not to supply every detail we would like, but He does supply every detail we need. The Bible was never meant to be a scientific textbook, listing all the facts, but a story communicating the important facts. Mark Twain said "It is not the things in the Bible I don't understand that bother me, it is the things I do understand." It is good to ask questions, but sometimes we need to realise that there will never be a satisfactory answer this side of heaven. All our questions, however, should be seen against the backdrop of God's sacrificial love in the death of His Son, Jesus Christ, and that He always seeks our best interest.

Gender Equality

FORUM VOICE

I don't understand why the serpent deceived Eve instead of Adam. Is there any significance behind the sequence of creation?

COVER TO COVER RESPONDS

Ladies First – Some people have used the creation sequence of man before woman and the temptation sequence of woman before man to propose a superiority and domination of men over women. Thank God that the New Testament shows us that we are joint heirs with Christ and that there is an equality between the sexes (Gal. 3:28).

An interesting verse in 1 Timothy 2:14 could be used to suggest that women are more likely to be deceived by temptation, but men are more likely to deliberately disobey God's Word. Remember however, that although Eve was Satan's target in Eden, it was a man, Judas, who was tempted to betray Jesus. It is important to realise that God often used women in positions of power and authority. For example, Deborah was one of the judges of Israel, Esther a queen whose intercession saved the Jews from extermination, Huldah a prophetess and in the New Testament women such as Phoebe, Chloe, Priscilla, Tryphena, Tryphosa, Persis and Nympha play a prominent role in the ministry of the early Church.

One of the quotes I like best is "Woman was made from man's side that she might walk beside him, not from his foot that he should step on her."

Noah and His Ark

FORUM VOICE
When Noah was instructed by God to move living things into the ark, were fishes included? If so, where were they kept for so long? If not, how come they died in their natural habitat – water?

FORUM VOICE
Just because nothing is mentioned about fishes, we can't simply assume that Noah didn't include them. I think Noah needed to drink when he is in the ark. So, why not a build a big acquarium – and keep fish in it?

FORUM VOICE
During the time in the ark no babies were born to Noah or his sons. They were in the ark long enough. Maybe God stopped their natural desire to reproduce, and the same in the sea. Thus reducing the numbers of fish.

FORUM VOICE
Does it really matter whether he took fish or not? Surely the important thing is that God is sovereign and He knows, so that's all that matters? Anyway fish can swim so they'd have been OK outside; except of course if the sea was salt and they were fresh water fish or the water was fresh and they were salt water fish!

FORUM VOICE
The Bible only mentions the destruction of the living things on the ground and the air. There's nothing mentioned about the fish.

ForumVoice

FORUM VOICE

I found this about Noah and the ark and thought it might help. Based on the size the Bible says the ark was, and on the number of species of animals, this really was not a problem. On the basis of volume, the ark was roughly equivalent to 522 railroad stock cars. A standard railroad stock car can carry 240 sheep. This means the ark could have carried 125,000 sheep. The average dry land animal is considerably smaller than a sheep, as there are only a few large animals. The ark was constructed in three storeys and each fitted with rooms or nests. So, how many animals were needed to fit in the ark? There are not very many species of mammals, birds, amphibians and reptiles. Ernst Mayr, the leading systematic biologist gives the number as 17,600. Allowing for two of each, we are only at 35,200. Let's assume we are out a bit in our calculations and two of each actually comes to 50,000. This is still far less than the 125,000 that could have easily been carried, so there was ample room for food storage and living space for Noah and his family. God knew how much space would be needed, and He provided.

Trials of Job

> **FORUM VOICE**
> Is it fair for Job's children to die? Job suffered but survived the severe testing. He was subsequently blessed. But the same cannot be said for his children.

> *COVER TO COVER* RESPONDS
> Compare Job 1:2 with Job 42:10–12. God doubled all Job's "possessions", except his children. Why? Because his children from the first reference who had died were actually alive in heaven for eternity. So, now that Job himself has died he is in heaven with fourteen sons and six daughters. The ones who died first just went to be with the Lord earlier than the rest and they have all been together now for thousands of years. When we see things from a human standpoint God sometimes appears harsh, but when we see from a divine eternal perspective we suddenly realise how truly wonderful He is.
>
> Job is one of the most beautiful examples of a continually repeating pattern of redemption throughout the Bible. That which was lost, broken, despised, hurt, destroyed, sick, forsaken, betrayed, rejected, injured, imprisoned, hopeless and even crucified, is, by faith, transformed into something loved, blessed, whole and glorified. It happened to Abraham, Jacob, Joseph, Moses, David, Daniel, Stephen, Paul and even Jesus. In a sense it happens to us when God steps into the mire of our pit of sin and lifts us out and cleanses us to a new life through faith in His Son. When we are in the midst of painful experiences it can be confusing and even depressing but when we reach the end of the story we suddenly realise that the bad things that happened, God worked for good.

On Reflection

- In what ways do you seek to apply God's Word to your everyday life and relationships? How can you make your life biblically relevant?

- Are there any lasting principles from Genesis that have had a particular impact on you?

- What lessons about temptation do you take from the fall of Adam and Eve?

- What do you understand about the character of God from the story of the Flood?

- Noah risked ridicule and humiliation for his faith in God's Word. In what way can you step out in faith and stand out for God today?

- How do you think that you might respond if you were in Job's position? How do you cope, and who do you run to, when faced with adversity?

- Do you, like Jacob, realise and value the importance of God's blessings?

- Do you, like Esau, put any physical pleasures before your spiritual obligations?

- Either from the Bible or from life, who is your example in the Christian faith and what positive impact have they made on you?

- Are there any areas of your life you need to lay on the altar before God?

CommentOn   *Cover to Cover* Forum

http://www.cover2cover.org/docs/forhome.htm

2

Second Things First

Exodus, not Genesis, is arguably, the first book of the Bible! To say this is to remind ourselves that what is revealed in Genesis was first given to Israel, to those ex-slaves delivered from tyranny in Egypt. It was in Israel that this revelation was cherished and preserved. In other words, Genesis is best viewed from the standpoint of the events recorded in Exodus.

From this perspective what we find in Genesis are answers to the kind of questions that would inevitably have arisen among these uniquely elected former slaves. Three questions at least spring to mind.

Firstly, how did we get into Egypt in the first place and why were we liberated? Chapters 12–50 of Genesis provide the answer to this question and is summed up in Exodus 2:24 as "God heard their groaning and he remembered his covenant with Abraham, with Isaac and with Jacob." The immediate pretext for the Exodus is the story of Joseph which explains why Abraham's descendants ended up in Egypt (Gen. 37–50). Beyond this stand God's original promises and foundational commitment to Abraham (Gen. 12).

Israel inherits this destiny which touches not only the world, but, even wider still, the whole of the created order.

God turns this relationship into covenantal partnership (Gen. 15) later re-iterating the promise to Isaac (Gen. 26:3–5), and Jacob (Gen. 28:13–14). God's promise is the thread that connects the patriarchal stories and governs the future beyond them, becoming "a power which shapes the course of history" (Paul and Elizabeth Achtemeier).

Insight

How God's promise works out through the vagaries of the participants' real-life stories makes for gripping drama. Will there, given Abraham and Sarah's age, be any descendant at all? (Gen. 12, 21). Will Abraham's wrong move (with Hagar to produce Ishmael) jeopardise God's plan? (Gen. 16). Will the son of promise survive? (Gen. 22). And what about the so-called "ancestress in danger" theme – the barrenness of Sarah, Rebekah (25:21), and Rachel (29:31)? Can the story outlive the fraternal rivalries – Isaac versus Ishmael, Esau versus Jacob, Joseph versus his brothers? Frequent famines threaten the plot (12:10; 26:1; 41:54; 47:13), but then one eventually sends the sons of Jacob to Egypt where a hostile Pharaoh enlists them as slave labour and where liberation begins. "You intended harm, God intended good" sums up the paradoxical providence of the Genesis story (50:20).

Imagine being exiled in Babylon when the Torah began to take shape.

The second question is why were we, Israel, exclusively chosen by God? Genesis 1–11 answers this question. Israel exists and is chosen for the sake of the whole world. Abraham is called from the world of nations (Gen. 10) to be the means of God blessing all nations (12:3). He leaves the city man is building (Gen. 11:5) to move in faith towards the city God is building (Heb. 11:10). There will be no way back to the Garden – only forward through redemption to the garden-city, home to an international multitude of Abraham's descendants (Rev. chs. 7, 21, 22).

Israel inherits this destiny which touches not only the world, but, even wider still – the whole of the created order. Preserved by God at the Flood, Noah and his family become down-payments on humanity's future on an earth, whose continued existence is guaranteed by covenant as the stage for God's redemptive work to be accomplished. So Israel becomes the sample new human race heading for the Promised Land – the microcosm of the renewed earth God has set His eyes on. So, in setting the scene for Abraham, Genesis 1–11 sets Israel on a world stage.

Insight

The third question is who is this God? The text of Genesis 12–50 highlights above all else the amazing grace of God in working out His purpose through the emotional resistance, and even moral failures, of His chosen partners in the venture. These are realistically noted but "the narrative is read to illustrate something entirely different: namely the faithfulness of God" (Brevard Childs). Genesis is not interested, nor should we be, in parading the patriarchs as spiritual or ethical models, but rather as reluctant heroes plucked from domestic obscurity to be key players in God's bigger story. What applied to them applies to Israel (Deut. 7:7–9).

God responds to the needy and oppressed, makes promises and keeps covenant.

Genesis 1–11 encapsulates Israel's joyous discovery that the God, who has redeemed them and covenanted with them at Sinai, is no mere tribal or ethnic or even national god, but is in fact the One Creator God of the whole world. Imagine being exiled in Babylon, when the Torah began to take shape, feeling the force of Genesis 1 as it counters rival Near Eastern versions of the world's origins and sharpens your sense of special identity as the people of the one true God in a pagan culture. Israel's God is the One who has chosen not to abort the creation experiment

Insight

at the Flood but reserves the resources to redeem what He has created. This God responds to the needy and oppressed, makes promises and keeps covenant and entertains redemptive intentions for all He has made which will in time bring the full glory of a new creation. "Who among the gods is like you, O Lord?" (Exod. 15:11)

From Slavery to Worship

God's grace initiates redemption

It is a mistake to offset a gracious New Testament against a legalistic Old Testament. As Exodus 1–18 demonstrates, Israel's life was founded on grace and redemption. God's love is compassionate in that He responds to the current plight of the children of Israel. God's love is covenantal in remembering His previous commitments to the patriarchs (Exod. 2:24). This listening, loyal love for the oppressed launches the series of judgments on an evil empire and the false religion which buttressed it (12:12). The blood of the lamb which "saves" the Israelite households is for ever commemorated in the Passover feast and re-enacted in the ongoing animal sacrifices. Even Israel's "fall" into sin with the Golden Calf finally results in only a further expression of God's grace and compassion (34:6–7). The groan of slavery is now the cry of freedom. From now on Israel sings "the song of a people who would not be slaves again" (15:1–18).

> **This is real freedom: from oppression into the service of God.**

Redemption implies relationship

Israel encounters the Living God speaking out of the fire of the mountain, just as He had spoken to Moses out of the burning bush. Moses is called to be God's agent of deliverance for those God terms "my people" (Exod. 3:7), His "treasured possession out of all the peoples" (19:5). Despite their idolatry with the "Golden Calf", Moses refuses to let God disown them (32:11–14).

Redemption language implies "ownership" and "belonging". But the freedom being granted here is very different

Insight

from the self-determined, freedom of individual choice so prized in the Western, consumer-orientated world. This is real freedom: from oppression into the service of God.

Israel is called God's "son": "Let my firstborn son go free" (4:22–23). This designation will one day devolve onto her king (2 Sam. 7:14) and will eventually mark out Jesus as the royal Son who lives out Israel's calling (Matt. 3:17; 4:3), succeeding in the test where nation and kings have failed. In Christ we can share Israel's destiny as the "nobodies who became somebodies", marching in the glorious freedom of the sons of God, led by the Spirit, towards the new world coming (1 Pet. 2:10; Rom. 8:18–25).

Relationship is sealed by covenant

Exodus takes the story of the Israelites from bondage to Pharaoh, to bonding with God (Exod. 19–24). The Sinai covenant mirrors closely the shape of those ancient suzerain-vassal treaties, which we know were drawn up between kings and their subjugated peoples. But this covenant is rooted in God's sovereign grace and redemptive initiative (19:4; 20:2). So why the law? The Law/Torah was not given so that Israel by good works could earn salvation; the law was given to a people already redeemed as the description of how a covenant people should live. This is a "law of freedom". It seeks to promote precisely that – a just, free, caring society which is the opposite of the slave-driven, oppressive society Israel suffered under while in Egypt.

> **Gentiles, who were once outsiders, are grafted in by faith and grace to the one covenant family of God.**

At Sinai another key link is forged in the great covenantal chain which runs through the whole Bible. Gentiles, who were once outsiders, are grafted in by faith and grace to the one covenant family of God (Eph. 2:11–22; Rom. 11:17; 1 Pet. 2:9).

Covenant implies partnership
Israel is commissioned at Sinai to be a "holy nation, a royal priesthood". Israel has a mediatorial role, the agency through which God's blessings flow to the world, and through which the world's sin finds its ultimate solution. For the world's sake, Israel must remain different from the world. Israel is called to live out the human role of image-bearers of God on the earth. So throughout Leviticus "Be holy, as I am holy" becomes Israel's "designer label".

Biblical worship is always a political act.

Priestly roles, sacrificial rites and complex rules of holiness – remote as they can seem to us – were all intended to maintain Israel's God-glorifying distinctiveness. For our part, in Christ, and empowered by the Holy Spirit, we can dare to be as different as God and so discover that the best way to serve the world is to be the Church.

Partnership makes worship a priority
"The book moves from the enforced construction of buildings for Pharaoh to the glad and obedient offering by the people of a building for the worship of God", writes Terence Fretheim. The Tabernacle is intended to be a portable worship sanctuary and since God is king it's a a royal palace, with the "ark of the covenant" (later called the "footstool of God's throne") as its focal point. Biblical

worship is always a political act since it asserts God's kingship over many rivals and idolatries.

Insight

The Tabernacle is also a symbolic counterpart to creation, (compare Exod. 39:43 with Gen. 1:31; Exod. 39:32 with Gen. 2:1). As the Sabbath day consecrates time, so the Tabernacle sanctifies space. Tabernacle worship declared that there is one place where God's creative order is restored, where His glory once more can rest (40:34). So our worship, in engaging the glory of God, may yet prove to be the "gravitational force" for the re-centring and re-ordering of God's fragmented world.

Moses

There are so many aspects to the life of Moses that it is impossible to sum them up in one short feature. Each reader will have their own particular favourite story about his life and character, but the Bible itself makes an astonishing claim about Moses when it refers to him as "a very humble man, more humble than anyone else on the face of the earth" (Num. 12:3). In other words the one characteristic that made him stand out from the crowd was not his bravery, determination, wisdom or leadership, but his humility.

This is a surprising claim for someone who personally ordered and led an execution of 3,000 of his own people (Exod. 32:25–28). Moses oversaw the destruction of Egypt, commanded the nation of Israel, directed their armies, judged the people, ordered the construction of the Tabernacle and ruthlessly put down insurrection; yet "he was more humble than anyone else on the face of the earth".

A dictionary definition of a humble person would include words such as unassuming, meek, subservient, obscure and someone who is always in the background rather than the forceful leader of a powerful nation. The Bible therefore must define a "humble" person in totally different terms to our own.

The Hebrew word for "humble" is *anayv* and is often used to describe the poor and those with a subservient attitude, particularly in comparison to those who are rich

and arrogant. "Humble" people see themselves as "second in line" and at the mercy of the decisions of those who rule over them. In Exodus 10:3, God says to Pharaoh, "How long will you refuse to humble yourself before me?" Although Pharaoh was a great and powerful ruler all his wealth and authority was nothing compared to God, yet in his arrogance he refused to acknowledge that God was greater and more powerful. Pharaoh could still have ruled Egypt by being humble enough to recognise that God was greater and obeying His command to "let the people go".

Moses was a humble man because he acknowledged and obeyed God in all his ways. Moses did not always agree with God, but he saw himself "second in line" and subservient to God's greater authority and wisdom. It was that attitude and his desire to be obedient that made Moses the most humble person on the face of the earth. There was no one else who so sought to obey and follow God all the days of his life, as a result Moses was given the accolade by God of "my servant" (Num. 12:1–8). The contrast with Miriam and Aaron is interesting because in Numbers 12 they sought after position and authority out of a sense of jealousy and personal selfish ambition to promote themselves, but they were not "humble" before God. Moses was humble before God and God gave him the position of authority.

In the New Testament, Jesus repeated this concept during his Sermon on the Mount when he said, "Blessed are the meek, for they shall inherit the earth". The meek here are not weak, frightened submissive people but those who instead submit themselves to God's reign over their lives, people who hunger and thirst for His righteousness and obey His command to go into all the world preaching the good news of salvation through faith in Jesus Christ. If we can truly understand the Bible definition of a humble person and seek to fulfil it ourselves, then perhaps we, like Moses, could be a powerful instrument in God's hands in our own land and time.

The Tabernacle

InDetail

The Tabernacle was a movable structure where God dwelt amongst the Israelites who were encamped around it. It consisted of an outer court made like a fence from linen hung between poles and was approximately 54 metres long by 27 metres wide and nearly 3 metres high. Inside this area towards the far end was a large tent of around 15 metres long, 3 metres wide and 3 metres high covered with various curtains and animal skins. The first section of the tent was the Holy Place, only accessible by the priests. A thick curtain called the veil stretched across the tent inside and separated the Holy of Holies, where only the high priest was allowed once a year on the day of Atonement.

The importance of the Tabernacle is its symbolism which was later used in the New Testament book of Hebrews to explain how and why guilty sinners can experience an intimate relationship with a holy God. The Tabernacle was laid out in such a way that it symbolises the path to relationship, then friendship and finally intimacy with God. It also speaks very clearly of Jesus. For example, the entrance to the outer court was called the Gate, the entrance to the Holy Place was called the Door and the entrance to the Holy of Holies was the Veil. Jesus is the Way (John 14:6), the Door (John 10:9) and the Veil (Heb. 10:19–20).

Brass Altar

This was made of wood overlaid with brass and was the place where sacrifices were made and then burnt. It stood immediately inside the Tabernacle and signified that the only way to a holy God was through a sacrifice for sin and without that sacrifice no further progress was possible. It speaks of the sacrifice of Jesus who was the

"Lamb of God, who takes away the sin of the world!"
(John 1:29). It was not just that a sinner made a sacrifice
but that the sacrifice was representative of the death of
that sinner in their offering. That offering had to be totally
pure, without blemish or sin (Lev. 1:2–4). The Brass Altar
was the place of all burnt offerings including those of
consecration or dedication.

Brass Basin

This was made from the mirrors of the Israelite women
(Exod. 38:8) and was filled with water. As the priests
looked into it they would immediately have seen anything
unclean and then washed themselves. It speaks of the
revealing (Jam. 1:23–25) and cleansing (Eph. 5:26) power
of God's Word. In John 15:22 Jesus spoke of the revealing
nature of His words and in John 13:1–10 and 15:3 He
spoke of their cleansing power.

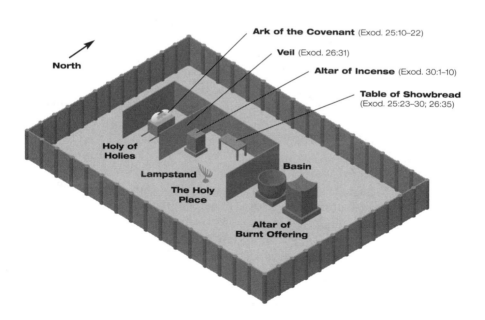

North

Ark of the Covenant (Exod. 25:10–22)

Veil (Exod. 26:31)

Altar of Incense (Exod. 30:1–10)

Table of Showbread
(Exod. 25:23–30; 26:35)

Holy of Holies

Lampstand

The Holy Place

Basin

Altar of Burnt Offering

Gold Lampstand

This was a seven-branched lamp which burnt oil to provide light in the otherwise dark interior of the Holy Place. The lampstand can be seen as referring to Christ, the Light of the World (John 8:12) and also to the Holy Spirit who is likened to oil burning from a seven-branched lamp (Zech. 4:2–6). Just as a single diamond can have many faces so in Isaiah 11:2 the Holy Spirit is seen to have seven aspects: wisdom, understanding, counsel, power, knowledge, fear of the Lord and the Spirit of the Lord.

Gold Table of Showbread

The purpose of the table was to display and "show" 12 loaves of bread before the Lord for seven days after which time the priests could eat them, replacing the bread with another 12 loaves. The bread was made with fine flour and is seen to signify a pure life and heart examined and approved by God. It speaks of communion where we break and eat the covenant bread at the "Lord's table" (1 Cor. 10:16–21). In this sense it speaks of Jesus who lived a pure life before God and whose body was broken for us that we might know the friendship and fellowship of the Father. Jesus is the "Bread of Life" (John 6:48–58). We too, however, are on display before God and subject to examination and the call to live a pure life (1 Cor. 11:23–31; Jer. 17:10; 1 Pet. 1:15–16).

Gold Altar of Incense

Incense speaks of prayer and praise (Rev. 5:8). The first altar of brass was for sacrifice but this one was for worship by which we draw near to God (John 4:24). As the place of prayer and intercession it reminds us of Jesus who is the mediator (1 Tim. 2:5) always making intercession for us (Heb. 7:25).

Ark of the Covenant

This was a wooden box overlaid with gold and contained a pot of manna, Aaron's rod that budded and the commandments written on the tablets of stone (Heb. 9:4). It speaks of Jesus who is the true manna from heaven (John 6:51), the fruitful Branch (Isa. 4:2, 11:1) and the Word of God (John 1:1).

Mercy Seat

This formed a lid for the open ark and was sprinkled with the blood of the atoning sacrifice by the high priest to obtain God's mercy. In Romans 3:25 Jesus is literally a "mercy seat" through faith in His blood. It was in a sense the throne of God for it was there that God was "seated" and met with His people (Exod. 25:22). Hebrews 4:16 encourages us to approach the throne of grace with confidence to receive mercy and grace in time of need.

InDetail

The Symbolism of the Rod

FORUM VOICE
In Exodus, why is the rod of Moses turned into a serpent when this is a symbol of evil, is there any significance behind it?

COVER TO COVER RESPONDS
We need to be very discerning when considering symbols in the Bible. For example, a lion could refer to Jesus (Rev. 5:5), the Devil (1 Pet 5:8) or an animal (Dan. 6:16). Also, the original language is very important, so in Genesis 3 the "serpent" in Hebrew is *nachash*, whereas in Exodus 7:9-10 the "serpent" is *tannin*, which is an island or sea monster. Some commentators suggest this could have been a crocodile.

Pharaoh's Hard Heart

FORUM VOICE
God foretold that Pharaoh's heart would be hardened. I don't understand why He wants to harden it. In every other verse, "But the Lord hardened Pharaoh's heart." Why did He have to do this? Doesn't Pharaoh have his own will on his own stubbornness?

FORUM VOICE
Initially Pharaoh hardens his own heart (7:13, 7:22, 8:15, 8:19, 8:32, 9:7). It is his choice. Even though many around him are saying "this is the finger of God" and similar comments, Pharaoh is hard. Only after Pharaoh does this many times does God harden Pharaoh's heart still further.

It seems clear that:
1. Pharaoh deliberately and consistently disobeyed God. It was his choice.
2. God had always known that this would happen.
3. God is king – even over the Evil One. We learnt this with Job.
4. If people turn away from God after He has revealed Himself to them then they end up in an even worse condition (Luke 11:24–27).

COVER TO COVER RESPONDS
Let's also remind ourselves just how hard and cruel Pharaoh's heart was already. He oppressed the Israelites into slavery and attempted to wipe them out by killing all the male babies. Pharaoh deserved God's judgment. Someone has said that God only hardens a heart that is already hard. Even when Pharaoh did let them go he changed his mind and brought about his own destruction in the Red Sea. I believe that if at any time Pharaoh had shown signs of repentance God would have spared Egypt further judgment just as He spared Nineveh in the book of Jonah. The comment from *Cover to Cover* (p.45) is worth repeating: "The more we resist God's Word and the more we refuse to do the divine bidding the more stubborn our hearts become. The tragedy is that, when we insist on having our own way, God may let us have it."

47

The Tabernacle

FORUM VOICE

I've found reading about the Tabernacle quite difficult, as I find the descriptions hard to visualise. However, what has blessed me has been the repeated references to the way everything was done as the Lord commanded Moses. This was obviously a great blessing to Moses himself as it is the first time it is recorded that he blessed the people on account of it!

FORUM VOICE

I just was reading today where Aaron was consecrated and in turn, he consecrated the Tabernacle and its various pieces. Can you imagine how he must have felt, as he performed these requirements for the first time. He must have felt so much awe for God and how he was cleansing all the people from their sin, but I would think he would be a little nervous too, in case he did something wrong as God wasn't giving the Levites/priests too much leeway for error in the sacrifice/Tabernacle end of things. Thank God for His mercy ... we can be forgiven for all our wrongs simply by claiming the blood of Jesus.

A Question of Intimacy

FORUM VOICE

I have a question about sex. I am, of course, referring to Leviticus 15:1–33. If a man and woman having sexual intercourse were considered to be ceremonially unclean and could not be around people for a period of 24 hrs, wouldn't Israel have been a very lonely people? Sex as part of marriage is part of everyday life in our society, and probably theirs. What was unclean about it, bearing in mind we are always told how God invented sex and it's a good thing. Also why was a woman "unclean" for longer if she had a girl? Does this make God a sexist?

COVER TO COVER RESPONDS

It certainly is a struggle for many to read. Yet it is full of spiritual truth developing a number of doctrinal and practical themes centring on questions of pardon for guilt and fellowship with God. It reveals how God in His grace accepts the death of a spotless substitute as the only payment for the penalty of sin.

We can only fully understand the necessity for the death of Jesus by reference to Leviticus. In essence, each of the offerings and feasts speak of Jesus. In particular the Passover and Day of Atonement portray aspects of our wonderful salvation. There are also many practical applications. For example, anything we offer to God in terms of our time, possessions or even our very selves must be from pure motives and not second best. Leviticus chapter 25 is really the basis for the campaign to relieve the debt of the poorest nations, it also mentions the practice of the isolation of contagious diseases that is still relevant today.

Why was a woman unclean longer when she had a female baby? I don't think we know yet, but I have a cutting from the *Daily Express* newspaper dated 10 December 1999 which quotes Hippocrates writing around 400 BC: "A mother carrying a female baby has a pale face, whereas if she is carrying a male baby she has a healthy tone to her skin." A survey in Sweden from 1987 to 1995 revealed more cases of morning sickness in mothers with female babies possibly because a female foetus has higher levels of a pregnancy related hormone called human chorionic gonadotropin. Maybe carrying a female foetus requires a longer recovery period? These are however only opinions and we must be careful not to always use the contemporary climate to judge biblical events.

FORUM VOICE

The question about sex (Lev. 15:18) bothers me too. On the surface, it makes sex (in a matrimonial relationship) look unholy. Yet the Bible says in Hebrews 13:4 (KJV) that "marriage is honourable in all, and the bed undefiled".

COVER TO COVER RESPONDS

The chapter and the uncleanliness is not really to do with the act of sex but of bodily discharges. So for example, a man who experiences a nocturnal emission of semen in verse 16 is unclean in the same way as a man and woman who have enjoyed sexual relations. In fact in verse 18 it seems that it is not the sex act but the emission of semen that causes the uncleanliness, ie a bodily discharge. Part of the issue here appears to be the elimination of the spread of possibly contagious bacteria that may be in the discharge or could breed if the discharge is not cleansed. For example in verse 13 washing is in RUNNING water not still water which could retain the bacteria. Also in verse 12 a clay pot which is porous has to be broken whereas a wooden pot need only to be rinsed. Similarly, in Numbers 19:11–12 a person touching a dead body is unclean and must wash in water. Three thousand years later in the 1840s Doctor Ignaz Semmelweis in Vienna speculated that the high mortality rates in his hospital could be due to the examination of living patients by physicians who had just completed the morning's autopsies of people who had died in the night. He instituted a procedure of hand washing similar to the Levitical rules and immediately the mortality rate dropped. His reward? Dismissal, because his colleagues hated to keep on washing their hands and the mortality rates went up again! I have in front of me a cutting from the *Daily Express* newspaper dated Monday 7 February 2000 which says and I quote, "Hospital infections could be killing as many as 5,000 National Health Service patients every year. Doctors are the biggest culprits for spreading bugs simply because they are not washing their hands between

treating patients, according to a new report."
Put Leviticus in a museum because it's so out of date?
No! Put it on hospital walls because it's so up to date!

FORUM VOICE
I figured it had to be something medical, but I guess I thought it referred to normal emissions of semen rather than the washing after sex (to prevent infections). I think that, in trying to understand God, we sometimes mistakingly view Him as a spoilsport for certain rules and regulations that we actually have no idea about. But because He is such a loving God these boundaries are there to protect us. I find that amazing.

The Punishment of Moses

FORUM VOICE

Why was Moses punished for "striking" the rock, rather than "speaking" to it? Moses did so many great things, and although he let God down occasionally God always forgave him. But he got punished for this offence. What was so unforgivable?

COVER TO COVER RESPONDS

The issue of Moses' sin and subsequent punishment of exclusion from the Promised Land is not an easy one. The text of Numbers 20:6–12 suggests three particular sins of Moses. The first is one of disobedience, the second one of unbelief and the third claiming honour that was due only to God for himself. Many of God's blessings are conditional on our obedience (Deut. 28), we cannot receive God's promises if we have a heart of unbelief (Heb. 3:12–4) and God will not share His glory with another (Isa. 42:8).

In Numbers chapter 20 (repeated in Deut. 32:48–52) there appears to be an issue regarding the fact that Moses did not "uphold the holiness of the Lord". Although this could be due to disobedience or unbelief, we could also consider the text of Psalm 106:32–33 which suggests that "trouble came to Moses" because of his "rash words" – and not simply the act of striking the rock. What were Moses' rash words? Numbers 20:10: "must WE bring you water out of this rock?" That is, Moses seems to claim the miracle as something he and Aaron did and in so doing both denied God the glory and honour for the miracle and took the honour for himself. God seems to take particular exception when people claim God-like honour and abilities for themselves. For example, He made Nebuchadnezzar insane (Dan. 4 and 5:18–21) and killed Herod (Acts 12:21–23).

On Reflection

- Which of the commandments do you find the hardest to keep? List them in order and pray that God helps you to deal with these issues.

- What can you do to contribute to the work of God in your locality?

- Do you need to change the way you manage your time and finances to give God what is due to Him?

- Identify the gifts God has given you and the people in your congregation for the building up of the church.

- How real a problem is jealousy in your life and the life of your church?

- Like everyone Moses had strengths and weaknesses, such as faith, compassion, prayer, determination, humility on the one hand and temper, anger, lack of delegation on the other. Do you share any of these aspects of character?

- Are you like Moses before the Red Sea facing an impossible situation that only prayer and God can change?

- Could you help your church leadership in some way and reduce the pressure they have to bear?

- How can you apply the lesson from Moses into your own life situations?

CommentOn   *Cover to Cover* Forum

http://www.cover2cover.org/docs/forhome.htm

3

Deuteronomy
– Jesus' Favourite Book

Deuteronomy has been aptly described as the heartbeat of the Old Testament. "Feel the pulse of Deuteronomy", urges Chris Wright, "and you are in touch with the life and rhythms of the whole Hebrew Bible." It is "one of the great theological documents of the Bible" concludes Gordon McConville.

Insight

In its final form Deuteronomy is presented to us as based on the final three addresses of Moses to the new generation of Israelites, who after the débâcle of the wilderness wanderings are now poised to enter the Promised Land across the Jordan from the East. Within this there is a simple past–present–future format: the story of the past (chapters 1–4), the shaping of the present (chapters 5–28), the securing of the future (chapters 29–32) – a simple pattern observed within individual sections like chapter 5.

> **Deuteronomy serves as a plumb-line against which the subsequent history of Israel is to be measured.**

This makes Deuteronomy very much a "boundary book", presenting the challenge to a people facing the death of Moses and standing at the frontier of a whole new phase of its existence. It offers a vision of life for Israel as God's people whose mission is to be a "holy nation" within a pagan environment. Will God's people succumb to the attractions of the surrounding culture? Or can they live differently? These are the questions posed by the book.

Insight

Deuteronomy is a "a pivotal book: it provides an interpretation to what precedes and what follows" (Terence Fretheim). It is "for a people on the move … as it moves into the future with God" (Chris Wright). The book therefore serves as a plumb-line against which the subsequent history of Israel is to be measured. So the narrative books which follow – Judges to 2 Kings – are often termed the Deuteronomic history. Neglect this charter for national faith and well-being and Israel drifts away from covenant; recover this book and revival ensues. If Deuteronomy – or some form of Deuteronomy – was in fact the law-book which King Josiah so dramatically rediscovered during his reign then we have a graphic illustration of the impact it can make (2 Chronicles 34–35).

The title of the book in English comes from the Greek version (LXX) of Deuteronomy 17:18 where the Hebrew speaks of a "copy of this law" which the LXX translated as "deuteronomium" or "second law". But to call the book "a second law" is potentially misleading because it is not a second law but a re-affirmation and expansion of the "first" law given at Sinai demanded by the occasion. And the occasion – as we have seen – is the renewal of the covenant with the new generation about to occupy the Land of Promise.

In this regard it is fascinating to see how Deuteronomy roughly matches in its structure the classic covenant-treaty form as used in the Ancient Near East. These "suzerain-vassal treaties" regulated the relationship between the King and his subjugated people and were arranged to a set formula to which the book of Deuteronomy approximates. These included:

● Preamble: identifying the participants (1:1–5)

- Historical Prologue: summarising the previous relations between the participants (1:5–4:49)

- General Stipulations: outlining the broad terms of the treaty (chapters 5–11)

- Specific Stipulations: offering detailed "case laws" to maintain the sanctity of the relationship (chapters 12–16 and basically following the order of the "ten words")

Insight

- Blessings and curses: describing sanctions and motivations (27–28)

- Witnesses: in this case "heaven and earth"! (30:19) and in future, the book itself (31:19,26) deposited as an official record and enshrined in song (31:21)

- Continuity provisions: including the amazing provision of hope beyond the "death" of the nation in Exile (chapter 30) and the more immediate transfer of leadership from Moses to Joshua (31:7–8; 14–15; 23; 34:9). The transmission of the oral Word of God to the written text of Torah (31:9–13; 31:24–29) and even the translation of Torah from prose into poetry (31:21; 32). In fact the Song of Moses itself can be broken down into these elements we have listed which parallel ancient suzerain-vassal treaties. This song serves as the foundational covenant lawsuit upon which subsequent prophetic lawsuits against Israel are drawn.

For this reason Deuteronomy consists largely of teaching material which Israel must learn and observe. Much of this takes the form of laws. But to think of "law" in strictly legal terms is to do less than justice to the rich concept of "Torah" which has the broader connotation of "teaching and instruction". Deuteronomy amounts to an

Old Testament "manual for discipleship" (Dennis Olsen), a religious text intended to shape a way of life for God's people.

With this in mind it is important to note how Deuteronomy – as with the wider Torah – is an "interweaving of law and narrative" (Fretheim). The obligations only make sense within the framework of a gracious story, a redemptive relationship. In other words, "the law does not stand as an external code but is integrated with Israel's ongoing story" (Fretheim). Obedience is not simply related to some rigid and fixed law but to the integrity of the story, so that God's people are enjoined never to forget who they are and are urged to live by this story and no other. This opens the possibility that law will need to be revised and re-applied, and even altered, in the light of new phases of the one story of the Creator God and His redeemed people. In fact, Deuteronomy is already evidence of this process at work (for example the laws on slaves in Exod. 21:1–11 with Deut. 15:12–18).

The obligations only make sense within the framework of a gracious story, a redemptive relationship.

Deuteronomy's memorable highlights include: the Shema (6:4), the basis for Israel's election being solely in love (7:7), the priority of living by God's Word (8:3), warnings against rebellion in the light of the Golden Calf apostasy (9:7), the three main temptations Israel was inclined to (7:17; 8:17; 9:7), the centrality of love and worship to the covenant relationship with God (10:12; 12:4), the promise of Rest as encapsulating the end of obedience (12:10), and the hope of a prophet like Moses arising (ch.18). The blessings and curses (chs.27–28) are not some technique for "health, wealth and prosperity" but the outcome of walking in covenant relationship with God (see Mark 10:28–31 with the bonus of added "persecutions").

The book may well contain – as conservative scholars suggest – a substantial core of Moses' teaching, adapted to later situations after influencing (or being influenced by) prophets like Jeremiah, and receiving final editorial shape at the time of the Exile ("as it is today" 29:27). It certainly anticipates the tragic end of the story in exile (ch. 30). Even then God will act in sovereign grace to restore His people beyond exile. Note, for example, how the command of 10:16 becomes a promise in 30:6. Chapter 30 is an extraordinary anticipation of the new covenant realities propounded later by Jeremiah and Ezekiel. In this future – beyond the efficacy it seems of the very sacrificial system laid down in the Torah – there is offered a daring new way of being God's people in the world. This will be based "not so much on human abilities and faithfulness as on the promise of God's faithfulness and God's active transformation of people and communities" (Dennis Olsen). As the title of Gordon McConville's helpful study of the book indicates, Deuteronomy offers "grace in the end".

Insight

> **Jesus, in effect, re-enacted Israel's story, being disciplined as Israel was in the wilderness as a "son" is disciplined (Deut. 8:5).**

Deuteronomy has been called Jesus' favourite book. His temptations in the wilderness, according to the Evangelists, mirrors the testing of Israel there, with His forty days deliberately evoking their forty years. And it is to Deuteronomy that Jesus turns for the charter for how

God's covenant partner should live. Jesus, in effect, re-enacted Israel's story, being disciplined as Israel was in the wilderness as a "son" is disciplined (Deut. 8:5). But He succeeds where Israel failed by holding fast to the Deuteronomic vocation (Matt. 4:1–11). As God's "Son" and faithful covenant Partner, Jesus, the True Israel, fulfils the Law. It is also worth noting another immensely important implication of this Deuteronomic identification of Jesus with Israel: the uniqueness of Jesus in a pluralistic world is rooted in Israel's own uniqueness among the nations (Deut. 4) and His embodying of that uniqueness.

Deuteronomy chapters 27–32 are an important seedbed of Paul's thinking, especially in Galatians 3 and Romans 9–11 where he presents Jesus as bearing the curse of exile and releasing the promised blessing of Abraham to the whole world.

The immediacy and challenge of Deuteronomy is felt by the reader through the repetition of "now" and "today" (5:1 etc.). The time-span of the Torah has embraced the immeasurable aeons of creation, the strange ages of the antediluvians, the longevity of the patriarchs, the "four hundred years" in Egypt, the forty years in the wilderness, and it's all come down to this, to this "now", to this "today" – the "eternal now", the crucial moment of choosing life or death. "Today if you will hear his voice"... Deuteronomy seems to plead with us. As Andrew Murray, spiritual sage of an earlier age, once said: "'Today' is the key to your failure: you waited for strength to make obedience easier and for feeling to make the sacrifice less painful."

A renewal of covenant vows in remembrance of Him brings the redemptive past into the vivid present, "It is not with our fathers that the Lord made this covenant, but with us, with all of us who are alive here today" (5:3). In an extraordinarily prophetic way this draws in the future also, "I am making this covenant … not only with you who are standing here with us today in the presence of the Lord our God but also with those who are not here today" (29:14). In the light of this, how might we keep the eucharistic feast, remembering until He comes?

As the "heartbeat of the Old Testament" Deuteronomy reminds us that law and covenant are metaphors describing the dynamics of our relationship with a living God. His voice speaks living words which are our food and drink, He invites us to love Him in return with passionate intensity and risk-taking faithfulness – and to start again "today".

Suggested Reading

Chris Wright, *Deuteronomy* in the NIBC series, published by Hendrickson 1996 (ISBN 0-85364-725-9)

Patrick Miller, *Deuteronomy* in the Interpretation series, published by Westminster/John Knox Press 1990.

Dennis Olsen, *Deuteronomy and the Death of Moses: Overtures to Biblical Theology*, Fortress Press 1994.

Bruce Birch, Walter Brueggemann, Terence Fretheim, David Peterson, *A Theological Introduction to the Old Testament,* Abingdon 1999.

Ruth

The story of Ruth illustrates the gospel in a nutshell. It is also a remarkable story of unsurpassed loyalty where commitment shines like a sparkling diamond against the darkness of betrayal and murder that so often characterised relationships in the Old Testament.

In Hebrew the word Ruth means "friend" or "associate". It is derived from the word for a shepherd and his flock and carries with it the sense of close companionship and support on a common journey. Ruth was from Moab, therefore an "outsider" to God's promises to the chosen nation of Israel. When her Israelite husband died she could have remained in Moab with her sister Orpah. Instead she chose to accompany her widowed mother-in-law, Naomi, back to Israel.

It is intriguing to compare Ruth with Orpah, who initially said she would go with Naomi and even kissed her. Eventually, however, she turned back to live amongst the familiar people and idolatry in the country of her birth. Ruth's words to Naomi are some of the most beautiful anywhere in Scripture, "Where you go I will go, and where you stay I will stay. Your people will be my people and your God my God. Where you die I will die, and there I will be buried."

Like Abraham before her, Ruth launched herself on a journey of faith to a distant land that she had never seen, but trusting in the God of whom she had heard, and come to believe in. Orpah sincerely offered Naomi her best wishes on a difficult and dangerous journey. Ruth faithfully offered Naomi herself.

The story of Ruth develops with God providentially arranging her marriage to Boaz. Ruth is redeemed from poverty, isolation and widowhood and becomes accepted as a member of a wealthy and powerful family amongst God's people. She is chosen by God to be an instrument of His purpose by which Jesus can be introduced into the world.

Like Ruth, we were once "strangers to God's promises" and ignorant of His love and mercy. Perhaps through unfortunate circumstances or the witness of others we embarked on a journey of faith that means we have to leave behind our old lives of sin and selfish thinking. We have been specially called by God to be a companion of Jesus to live a new life amongst others who also know Him. We have been adopted as sons and daughters into the royal family of heaven with God as our Father. The new kingdom we find ourselves in is at first strange and sometimes frightening but as we faithfully and obediently follow His directions God blesses us and we become an instrument through whom Jesus is introduced to the world.

Ruth is also a wonderful example of real friendship. In an age where many relationships break down her loyalty and total commitment to Naomi is a perfect illustration of true dedication whatever the cost. Ruth's relationship with Naomi was not based on shallow convenience or expediency, but on unshakeable principles of covenant commitment. Jesus put it this way, "Greater love has no-one than this, that he lay down his life for his friends" (John 15:12).

This is the depth of love and faithfulness that Jesus calls

us to emulate, "By this all men will know that you are my disciples, if you love one another" (John 13:35). Let the story of Ruth challenge and inspire you to be an obedient worshipper of God and a faithful friend to others.

Idolatry

FORUM VOICE
I am being really challenged about simplifying my life, and as I have worked on removing a lot of things from my life, I have experienced a joy and release from which I now realise were idols. For example, I had accumulated a vast amount of craft materials in my desire to be creative. This may sound harmless, even a good thing to desire, but it was the depth of that desire that was wrong. I so wanted to be good at all these different crafts, and dreamed of rooms full of my own creations. But now I realise that I do not have to prove myself in this way. I have spent so much time – not to mention money – in these pursuits, in many instances not actually achieving anything at all because I was often too anxious to persevere when I didn't meet with immediate success. It is all so illogical, I see that now. I think that, although I was a believer, I was not walking close to God, and did not have the security of knowing that He loves me "just as I am", but was continually thinking that I had to strive for approval. Now I realise that this is not so, and if I want to produce a craft item, I will do so for pleasure and relaxation, and certainly not put it before God.

COVER TO COVER RESPONDS
Someone on the *Cover to Cover* online forum suggested that the things they turn to in times of stress (TV, alcohol etc) had become her idols because they gave her a sense of peace apart from God. It is an interesting perspective on idolatry which may be more than simply worshipping a false image of a god. In *Every Day with Jesus* Selwyn Hughes wrote, "If God is not at work in our souls, pouring his life-giving water into us, then we look for some immediate form of gratification, something that will bring a cool taste to our parched spiritual tongues. It can come from anything; an affair, drugs, obsessions, pornography, promiscuity or even living off our professional expertise or gifts. These things have the same effect on our souls as crack cocaine on the body. Once we allow our hearts to indulge in these things, to bring false comfort to our souls, they can soon overpower our will." In short we can find other comforters and develop a reliance on our own abilities and resources or even the wisdom and resources of

others rather than God. The more wealthy we are, the more likely we seem to fall into this trap, which God specifically warned His people about and even gave them a festival to remember that God was their only true source of strength (Deut. 8). We are to live in the world and enjoy its beauty and benefits but we are not of it in the sense that we do not ultimately rely on it for fulfilment.

Sacrifice

FORUM VOICE

What's the difference between an offering and a sacrifice? Once some animals so loved their farmer that they decided to give him a surprise breakfast. The cow offered to give milk, the hens offered the eggs and the pig the bacon. The pig commented to his friends "You are giving an offering but I'm making a sacrifice". While understanding this difference I cannot see how to apply it in my life. I feel this refers to more than letting the old self die and living a new spiritual life in Christ. Where's the sacrifice in my life?

FORUM VOICE

An "offering" appears to be a gift in your illustration; while the "sacrifice" called for commitment and surrender. I think when we come to the Lord Jesus and surrender our lives at salvation that this is the first step. Letting the old self die and living a new spiritual life in Christ is what is expected next and is a commitment. This we can do only with God's help, which He gives to us through the Holy Spirit. In reality however this is an ongoing process and lasts our whole life, it is what sanctification is all about. Each day is an adventure, so begin it with Him. Sacrifice comes in different ways – giving up things that don't honour Him; disciplining our time; doing only what pleases Him; giving up the world's standards. It may be hard at first and will call for surrender and commitment, but as we keep at it soon it will be second nature to us.

FORUM VOICE

I'm a bit uneasy about animal sacrifices. Why did God, who put Adam in charge of taking care of His creation, allow him to slaughter animals in a ritualistic way to help His cause? I wonder about the historical context of all this – could it be that getting the Israelites to offer animal sacrifice was the only way of getting through to the people of that time that God had power over life and death?

COVER TO COVER RESPONDS

In Leviticus God is revealing the effect of sin and its remedy. Basically sin is a rejection of God and God acts entirely justly when He punishes the sinner. Because God

is a perfect Judge He cannot let sin go unpunished. The punishment of sin is death (Gen. 2:17, Rom. 6:23) and without such a death there is no cleansing of sin (Lev. 17:11, Heb. 9:27). God's revelation in Leviticus is that in mercy He will accept the death of a perfect substitute in the place of the sinner who would then be accepted back into fellowship with God so we could be at-one with Him. No human is perfect or without sin (Rom. 3:23; 1 Kings 8:46a; 1 John 1:8) and so God accepts an animal with no defects as an acceptable (temporary) substitute. The sacrificial killing of an animal is signified by its body burnt on the Brazen Altar and its blood poured or sprinkled. In Leviticus 1:4 when the person making the offering lays his hands on the animal he is not just transferring sin from himself to the animal and the animal's purity to himself, but he is also identifying with the animal such that when the animal dies he also "figuratively" dies. This is consistent with the NT revelation that we died in Christ (Gal. 2:20; Rom. 6:6). Animals could never really take the place for human sin, only "cover" it and so Christ came as a fully perfect man and fully perfect God to die in our place (2 Cor. 5:21; Heb. 10:1–22; Isaiah 53). This is the doctrine of substitutionary atonement.

FORUM VOICE

Regarding unease towards animal sacrifices – I try to remember that God actually made the first animal sacrifices. Remember way back in the Garden of Eden, when Adam and Eve committed their sin, and when God found them, they were hiding because of their nakedness. Before God expelled them from the Garden, He gave them clothing, furs and pelts, to wear. In a Bible study I was told that God had to kill the animals to obtain this and therefore He made the first sacrifice using animals ... What He won't do for us to remove our sins!

FORUM VOICE

I once read there can't be any forgiveness or atonement of sin without the shedding of innocent blood. That is why the perfect Lamb of God, without any sin, our Lord Jesus shed His blood for us. Once and for all – we don't need to slaughter animals again.

The Saddest Story

FORUM VOICE
Why did the Levite give his concubine? Surely he knew what would happen, the mob weren't going to have an intellectual discussion with her. Is this story meant to illustrate the weakness of the Levite?

COVER TO COVER RESPONDS
Judges 19:1–21:25 – In the "ancient" East hospitality was very important and guests may be given the best of anything (indeed, many of us have slept on a sofa and given our bedroom to our guests). To dishonour a guest was a terrible offence. Both Lot and the house owner would rather offer their virgin daughters than allow their (male) guests to be violated. In Sodom the angels intervened, but here the man gave his (previously unfaithful) concubine to try to satisfy the lusts of the mob and preserve the lives of everyone in the house. Neither the mob nor the man acted honourably, but it seems he never expected them to kill her and was outraged at their actions.

I think that this story is one of the saddest in Scripture. Like the story of Sodom it illustrates the absolute depravity of mankind when, to fulfil perverted sexual lusts, they would kidnap, abuse and murder total strangers. Notice that the passage referred to above begins and ends with the phrase "Israel had no king" and Judges 21:25 concludes "every one did as he saw fit". There was no effective righteous leadership or respect of God and His laws. It took this horrible incident and its gruesome publicity of body parts dispatched to each tribe for the nation to realise and act against the depravity that was infesting the country. Eventually sin is judged so Sodom and Benjamin were destroyed because of their own godlessness.

Ruth

FORUM VOICE

I just had revelation – I could never understand why Ruth was so committed to Naomi, even being prepared to leave her own people. But it now dawned on me that it was when she found Naomi's God that she made Naomi's people her own. Leaving her natural family for God's people. I must say, I sometimes feel more at home with my new family in Jesus than my natural family too.

FORUM VOICE

Indeed, I think Ruth is also a woman of faith, and obedience. This can be seen when she left her home town and went to the unfamiliar land of Israel, and how she obediently followed the instructions of Naomi. In the end, she is greatly blessed. Does this show us a picture of how we should be before God? "Trust and obey, for there's no other way."

On Reflection

- Do you think Christians should give a tenth of their income as they did in the Old Testament?

- What do you think are our daily duties to God?

- Outline the personal, spiritual and social consequences of keeping or breaking each of the Ten Commandments.

- Recount instances of God's power and deliverance in your own life.

- Is there a personal "Jordan river" barrier in your life that you need to cross by faith?

- Is there a Jericho in your life or the life of your church that is stopping spiritual progress?

- What things do we need to drive out of our lives in order to fully enjoy God's provision for us?

- Are you bitter about some of your experiences or do you believe God can use them for good?

- Orpah lovingly kissed Naomi but would not leave her own people, however Ruth faithfully went with her and left everything else behind. Do you think you would be prepared to make such a sacrifice?

- How can you apply the lesson from Ruth into your own life situations?

CommentOn   *Cover to Cover* Forum

http://www.cover2cover.org/docs/forhome.htm

4

War and Peace –
Joshua and Judges

As young person I was gripped by a book called *The Struggle for Europe* by Chester Wilmot, a journalist's vivid account of how the Allied armies fought to help end World War II. Wilmot's book was intriguingly sub-titled: "How we won the war but lost the peace." This could be an appropriate sub-title for Joshua and Judges: How Israel won the war (Joshua) but lost the peace (Judges).

Let's start with the big picture to see the way that the Old Testament is shaped:

Genesis Exodus–Deuteronomy	Joshua > 2 Kings 1350 BC to 586 BC	Prophets
Pre-history, Patriarchal history Covenant and Law (= "Torah")	"Former Prophets"	"Later Prophets"
Part One fixes Israel's identity as God's redeemed and covenant people (re-established Deuteronomy)	**Part Two** shows how well or badly Israel (and her kings) kept covenant with God in the Land (hence Joshua to 2 Kings is called the "Deuteronomic history")	**Part Three** records the messages of the prophets who proph- esied during Part Two, calling on people and kings to return ("repent") to covenant faithfulness.

Insight

Joshua–Judges is an account of how Israel conquered and possessed the land of Canaan from its entry under Joshua (c.1400 BC) until its first king, Saul (1050 BC). For modern readers, God's conquest of Canaan is often a major moral problem. Is God guilty of arbitrary ethnic cleansing? There is no glib answer to this question but a number of considerations can be offered.

Joshua is connected to the larger story told in the Torah, reaching back to Genesis 1–11; it is therefore presented to us as part of the story of how God re-conquered a portion of the earth which belonged to Him from creation, reclaiming it from the rebellious and idolatrous powers of this world.

Discoveries from late Bronze Age (1500–1200 BC), especially at a place called Ugarit (modern Ras Shamra) on the northern coast of Syria, lead some scholars to believe that Canaanite culture was degraded, immoral, bestial, pagan, involving sacral prostitution and child sacrifice among other things (Lev. 18:24–28). If this is true then such a culture was finally reaping its judgment.

If we ask another question: "Does God hate sin this much?" – the answer must be "Yes!" But bear in mind that according to the Torah we can ask another question: "Does His patience run this far?" For an answer to this read Genesis 15:16. Joshua certainly presents the conquest to us as God's "holy war" (e.g. Josh. 5:2–15) with Israel as His army and the "spoils" could not be plundered as booty, instead they were placed under a "ban", that is they belonged exclusively to God.

One thing we must say in the light of the Cross is that since then God has sheathed His "sword" until the last and final day of reckoning (Rev. 19:15–21). One scholar's view is worth quoting: "The conquest was not the grossest injustice but God's highest justice … everyone of Yahweh's victories over His enemies in the process of history is a partial portrayal of His victory over all His enemies at the consummation of history" (Dale Ralph Davis, *No Falling Words* Baker, 1988).

In the longer view, any moral ambiguity attaching to God as a result of such accounts leads us to marvel at the condescension and humility of this God who chooses to put His reputation as a good and just God on the line. This same God is not afraid of "getting His hands dirty" and becoming intimately involved with a primitive people. His story is inextricably bound up with ours. Similarly, His plans have our grubby fingerprints all over them, but even at the risk to His image God refuses to disengage with history.

It's also worth pointing out that Judges illustrates the failure to fully occupy the land, so the view of some historians that the Conquest may never actually have taken this violent course may be on target. In any case, the Conquest was a "one-off" event. Israel-in-the-Land was a unique experiment, with the people given a unique chance to show how blessed it is to live "theocratically", i.e. under God's direct rule. Judges shows us how Israel lived up to this destiny.

David

BibleLives

Our world today seems to be obsessed with measurements and scientific facts. Some of our best selling books contain nothing but details of nature and records of human achievements. Our computers have an apparent infinite ability to store, analyse and reproduce data that would take a million lifetimes to read. In the midst of this insatiable thirst for information the story of David reminds us that there are some things which are totally beyond the capacity of mere mankind to measure.

When Samuel was told by God to anoint one of Jesse's sons to become king, he fell into the same trap of relying on his physical senses and measuring whoever came before him. The first son was called Eliab, which in Hebrew means, "whose father is God". Eliab was the oldest, he had the right name and when Samuel saw his height and physical appearance, he thought, "Surely this is the man the Lord has chosen!" (1 Sam. 16:6 TLB). God's response to Samuel is so instructive and helps reveal to us the true nature and perfect judgment of an all-seeing God, "Don't judge by a person's face or height, for this is not the one. I don't make decisions the way you do! People judge by outward appearance, but I look at a person's thoughts and intentions" (TLB).

Eventually after seven sons passed before Samuel, the prophet asked Jesse if he had any more children. It is interesting that even though Samuel had invited Jesse and his sons to the sacrifice, David had been overlooked as he was too young and only useful enough to watch the

sheep. It was David however whom the Lord had chosen
and he was anointed by Samuel. This is reminiscent of
the prophecy and life of Jesus for "in our eyes there was
no attractiveness at all, nothing to make us want him.
We despised him and rejected him ... and we didn't care"
(Isa. 53:2–3 TLB). "The same Stone that was rejected by
the builders has become the Cornerstone, the most
honoured and important part of the building" (1 Pet. 2:7
TLB). People measured Jesus as an ignorant carpenter
and David as an insignificant shepherd boy but in reality
both were anointed and empowered by the almighty,
invisible God.

Soon after his anointing by Samuel, we are presented
with perhaps the most famous story of David's life, when
he defeated Goliath as reported in 1 Samuel 17. Again we
have a picture of people looking only at external appear-
ances. The whole army of Israel including king Saul
looked at the giant Goliath and were terrified.

David brought supplies to his brothers who were in the
army and simply saw a tall man defying a giant God.
When David voiced his thoughts most of his fellow coun-
trymen saw a small weak boy and despised him. Saul
recognised the invisible but powerful anointing of God
upon David and allowed him to fight Goliath. David's
shout to Goliath reveals the falsehood of scientific
measurement. Goliath was a physical giant with a huge
sword and spear but little David with only a few stones
possessed the immeasurable power of a mighty God.
David cried out, "I come to you in the name of the Lord
... [God] works without regard to human means!
He will give you to us!" (1 Sam. 17:45, 47 TLB).

If we are to be mature believers we need to measure
people and situations according to the invisible spiritual

dimensions that can only be seen by eyes of faith. We too may seem insignificant and powerless according to the world's measuring systems but the truth is that the same Spirit that raised Christ from the dead now lives in us (Rom. 8:11). With God on our side we can overcome both our own inadequacies and every form of opposition because we come against them in the name of the Lord, who always leads us in triumphal procession in Christ (2 Cor. 2:14). Hallelujah!

The Book of Psalms

The Book of Psalms is one of the most read and loved books in the Bible and includes the famous "Shepherd Psalm", or Psalm 23, which even many non-churchgoers can quote. In Hebrew the title of the book is *Sepher Tehillim* (The Book of Praises) but our English title of Psalms comes from the Greek, *Psalmoi* (Songs). It is in fact a collection of 150 spiritual songs or poems written by a number of different authors such as David (73), Moses (1), Heman (1), Ethan (1), Asaph (12) and Solomon (2), including around 50 without the writer's name.

The human body contains various interconnected but totally separate systems such as the respiration, circulation, reproduction, digestion and nervous systems. We cannot understand the whole without first understanding the various parts. In the same way the one book of Psalms contains a variety of different subjects such as teaching, prophecy, penitence, God's character, thanksgiving and lament. For example, included within the Psalms are 128 facts about the Messiah and 72 facts about Judas. This illustrates the prophetic nature of the book and indeed a number of psalms are classified as "Messianic", for example Psalm 22 which prophesies Jesus' crucifixion, Psalm 24, 47 and 68, His ascension, and Psalm 45 the marriage of the Bride of Christ.

Expressing Emotions
Many Psalms are not to do with praising God but contain outpourings of emotions such as repentance (Psalm 51), desperation (Psalm 70), depression (Psalm 88), vengeance (Psalm 58), confusion (Psalm 73) and even homesickness (Psalm 137). There are, of course, also Psalms of praise (Psalm 150), joy (Psalm 100) and thanksgiving (Psalm

105). Perhaps two key references are Psalm 32:3–5 and Psalm 39:2–3 which both speak of an inner release and personal development when emotions are allowed to be expressed to God.

Many Christians think that God is only interested in their praises and does not want to hear about their fears, doubts and sorrows. They bury these emotions in an attempt to deny them, but when we bury an emotion we bury it alive. It keeps working deep within our personality until its acid weakens our faith or like a volcano we erupt without warning and harm or even destroy those closest to us.

The Book of Psalms shows us that God is vitally interested in our negative emotions and in fact delights when we are real with Him because it is then that He can help us. A number of the psalms show an emotional journey from fear to faith, confusion to confidence and guilt to glory, but the process can only take place when we take the first step of expressing those feelings to God. For example in Psalm 73 Asaph is grieved and embittered at the prosperity of godless people but when he expresses that to God he realises true wealth is only found in a relationship with God. In Psalm 13 David moves from the hopelessness of depression to hope in a God of salvation. Psalm 77 starts with "a soul refusing to be comforted" but ends with the assurance of God's overwhelming peaceful presence.

It is good practice to use the Book of Psalms to fulfil the recommendation in James 5:13, that if we are happy we should sing songs of praise and if we are in trouble we should pray. Find a psalm describing your painful emotions and by reading, prayer and meditation use it to express those feelings to God who can then help your own journey to faith and wholeness. Alternatively, find a psalm describing the positive emotions you feel or desire such as trust or peace and use it to develop those qualities in your own heart. Surgeons graft new skin on to someone who has been severely damaged. Similarly, we can graft the strengthening Word of God to repair and renew our own damaged emotions. It is this engrafted Word that can help to save our souls and bring us to maturity (Jam. 1:21 KJV).

Hebrew Poetry

As a book of poetry the psalms often employ the Hebrew technique of parallelism, which involves "rhyming" ideas rather than sounds. Usually this is found in two consecutive lines of verse, which complement, emphasise and explain each other. For example, Psalms 1:1–2, 3:1, 25:4, 42:1, 95:1, 2, 3, 4, 5, 6, 7, 8–11. Hebrew poetry also extensively uses dramatic figures of speech, which are found throughout the Bible and particularly in Psalms, for example:

Simile – a comparison of two things that resemble one another (Psalms 1:3–4; 131:2)

Metaphor – a comparison where one thing is declared to be another (Psalms 23:1; 84:11)

Implication – a comparison where the name of one is used in place of the other (Psalm 22:16)

Hyperbole – exaggeration for emphasis (Psalms 6:6; 78:27)

Rhetoric – questions to confirm or deny a fact (Psalms 35:10; 56:8; 106:2)

Metonymy – one noun used instead of another (Psalms 18:2; 57:9; 73:9)

Anthropomorphism – ascribing to God human characteristics to illustrate truth (Psalms 11:4; 18:15; 31:2)

Zoomorphism – ascribing to God animal characteristics to illustrate truth (Psalms 17:8; 36:7; 91:4)

Personification – ascribing human characteristics to lifeless objects (Psalms 77:16; 96:11–13)

Apostrophe – addressing lifeless objects (Psalm 114:5)

Synecdoche – representation of the whole by a part or vice versa (Psalm 91:5)

Hebrew poetry occasionally uses acrostics where consecutive letters of the alphabet commence each line or section. Psalm 119 is the most well-known example of this technique.

Structure
In rabbinical literature the Midrash says, "Moses gave to the Israelites the five books of the Torah (Law); and corresponding with these David gave them the five books of the Psalms". The psalms are not arranged chronologically otherwise Psalm 90 written by Moses, would be first. The psalms are grouped according to their content, so each group of psalms relates to each Book of the Torah.

Genesis
Psalms 1–41 concern humanity's relationship with God. In Psalm 1 obedience brings blessing, while in Psalm 2 disobedience brings ruin. In Psalms 16 and 22 we are introduced to the sacrificial death of the Son of Man.

Exodus
Psalms 42–72 concern the nation of Israel, especially
its ruin, redeemer, and redemption, with new promises
for the land (e.g. Psalm 69:35–36).

Leviticus
Psalms 73–89 concern the sanctuary as the place of
wisdom and worship in the presence of God. The sanctuary, congregation, assembly or Zion are referred to in
nearly every psalm. Psalm 84 expresses desire for God's
house.

Numbers
Psalms 90–106 concern Israel and the nations of the earth
and relates to the wanderings in the wilderness where
rebellion will bring punishment but faithfulness will result
in blessings (Psalm 101:6). The nations will come to know
and worship the God of the whole earth (particularly
Psalms 96–101).

Deuteronomy
Psalms 107–150 concern the Word of God. Disobedience
to the Word began humanity's sorrows, Israel's dispersion,
the sanctuary's ruin and earth's miseries. This section
begins with "He sent His word and healed them" (Psalm
107:20 NKJ) and includes the longest psalm, Psalm 119,
which focuses on the blessings of obeying God's Word.

The Book of Psalms concludes with five psalms ending
in "Hallelujah" – meaning "praise the Lord" – with the
final verse of Psalm 150 reading, "Let everything that has
breath praise the Lord. PRAISE THE LORD!"

Jephthah's Hasty Vow

FORUM VOICE

I think Jephthah was rather rash or hasty in making his vow of sacrifice. A vow is a freewill offering. It is self-imposed. God does not force anyone to make a vow. But once made, one is bound by it. Numbers 30:2 makes it clear: "If a man vow a vow unto the LORD, or swear an oath to bind his soul with a bond; he shall not break his word, he shall do according to all that proceedeth out of his mouth." Jephthah's case teaches us to be careful about what comes out of our mouth either during prayer or generally even in everyday conversations. Careless words could be very expensive. No wonder James (3:6) described the tongue as "a fire".

FORUM VOICE

Despite his hasty vow, I like and respect Jephthah for one thing – he had a very good sense of history. To the children of Ammon who were going to repossess all their lands from Israel, Jephthah recounted the historic facts of the case and concluded: "Will you not take what your god Chemosh gives you? Likewise, whatever the LORD our God has given us, we will possess" (Judg. 11:24). Unlike Jephthah, the children of Ephraim forgot the works of the Lord and were defeated in the day of battle (Ps. 78:9–11).

The devil is fond of trying to dispossess us of our inheritance in many subtle but sometimes violent ways. Like Jephthah, we need to stand firm, resist, and remind him of the victory of our Lord over him at Calvary. I believe those of us involved in *Cover to Cover* are developing the necessary "sense of history" to win the battles of life.

I do think Jephthah was incredibly rash and can't imagine anyone saying they would sacrifice the first thing coming out of his front door on his arrival back. Who did he think would come out of the door?! The family's pet fattened calf? God never endorsed a human sacrifice (He condemned societies who did sacrifice their children to destruction). If Jephthah had any sense he would have gone to God to find out what he should do and God would undoubtedly have revealed another solution.

Bible scholars believe that Jephthah's daughter was not killed as a sacrifice because human sacrifice was forbidden, but rather the vow was fulfilled in that she was dedicated to the service of the Lord and in particular she was dedicated to perpetual virginity. This is indicated in Judges chapter 11 verses 37–39 which conclude "and she knew no man" (KJV) or "and she was a virgin" (NIV) (for the rest of her life). It may be that she served the priests until she died. This was a serious issue for Jephthah himself because she was his only child and therefore his family line died.

Jephthah is another example of an imperfect person whom God could use. His mother was a prostitute, he was rejected by his brothers and he did some silly things, but overall, he was prepared to obey God and keep his promises. Jephthah is specifically mentioned as a person of faith in Hebrews 11:32. If God could use Jephthah then surely He could also use us.

FORUM VOICE
This then also explains why (Judg. 11:37) she wanted two months to bewail her fate with her girl friends. She wanted moral support to work through this "sentence" before she served it. I say "sentence" because she did not originally choose to live like a nun. She wanted her father to honour his vow. I think we can also learn from her total obedience and the way she deals with her pain before she goes into her ministry. That way she could consecrate her life and serve God obediently and not harbour resent-ment.

David and Saul

FORUM VOICE

While reading the story of Saul and David, I couldn't help noticing that Saul's behaviour was quite funny. Imagine allowing a boy of David's age to go and fight with Goliath! A battle that an army of grown men were too scared to fight. Saul is a good example of why we should be obedient to God. My pastor says God has a sense of humour and I believe it. It must have been some sight!

Something that baffles me is that after Saul's bout with the evil spirit, in 1 Samuel 19:23–24, the Spirit of God once again came upon Saul and he prophesied. But after that, he seemed to just return to his old ways. What was God's purpose for that incident?

FORUM VOICE

The Spirit of God that came upon Saul in Naioth, Ramah (unlike in earlier cases) was not for His glorification, nor does it signify the acceptance of Saul by God; the purpose was to "arrest" him. Earlier, Saul had sent his messengers (on three different occasions) to arrest David. They were also arrested by the Spirit of God. Saul should have therefore seen the hand of the Almighty in this. In his decadent state of mind and spirit, he failed to realise that God was at work. Instead, he chose to effect the arrest himself – a shameful degradation of the office of a king! David was able to run to safety while Saul and his arresters were themselves still arrested. There is nothing God cannot do to safeguard the interest of His servant.

I think is important that we learn a few lessons here. David was secure in spite of all the strategies of Saul and his host of spies because he trusted in God and his hands were clean. He also ran into the house of God or if you like, church. He ran to the man of God and trusted God for his safety. There is no better place to run to when in trouble. There, we will be safe under the shadow of the wings of the Lord. Where do we run to when we are in trouble?

Samuel

FORUM VOICE

Is it the real Samuel's soul or an evil spirit that was brought up by the woman in 1 Samuel 28:7-19? One leader in my Bible Study group told me that it was an evil spirit because God has clearly forbidden divination. However, as I read the Bible it sounds like the real Samuel's soul because the Bible does not say otherwise.

FORUM VOICE

The NIV Bible Study Notes for 1 Samuel 28:12, which is relevant to the above issue, reads like this: "The episode has been understood in many different ways, among them the following: 1. God permitted the spirit of Samuel to appear to the woman. 2. The woman had contact with an evil or devilish spirit in the form of Samuel by whom she was deceived and controlled. 3. By using parapsychological powers such as telepathy or clairvoyance, the woman was able to discern Saul's thoughts and picture Samuel in her own mind. Whatever the explanation of this mysterious affair, the medium was used in some way to convey to Saul that the impending battle would bring death, would dash his hopes for a dynasty and would conclude his reign with a devastating defeat of Israel that would leave the nation at the mercy of the Philistines, the very people against whom he had struggled all his years as king. And this would come, as Samuel had previously announced 'because of his unfaithfulness to the Lord.' "

On Reflection

- Like Hannah, are you deeply troubled by a problem that you need to pour out to God?

- Like Samson, do you have a weakness which robs you of the power of God?

- Like Saul, do you lack patience and in panic do things you shouldn't instead of waiting for God?

- Do you retaliate when people hurt you, or like David with Saul, do you leave justice to God?

- Are there any Goliaths in your life that you need to overcome?

- Saul's character had many flaws, including inferiority, jealousy, insecurity, disobedience, covetousness and fear. Do you share any of these characteristics. God can release you from them.

- Do you need to repent of any dealings with mediums, astrology, fortune telling or spiritualism?

- Can you be a friend to someone and give encouragement in their walk with God as Jonathan did with David?

- What is your favourite praise psalm, hymn or song? Why does it mean so much to you?

CommentOn *Cover to Cover* Forum

http://www.cover2cover.org/docs/forhome.htm

5

The Historical Books

Biblical history is a strange mixture: a boy prophet hears voices in the night; an old man falls off his chair and breaks his neck; there are witches and mediums; a guitar-strumming shepherd is summoned to be king; a pygmy beats a giant in a head-to-head contest; two men love each other deeply but are not homosexual; a royal pretender becomes target practice for an enraged spear-throwing king who's past his sell-by date; a monarch feigns madness and then shows kindness to the disabled; there are generals wanting to be president, femme fatales, floating axe-heads, economic expansion, hyper-inflation, prophets, politicians, refugees, spin-doctors, hangers-on, peasants, holy men, courageous women, civil war and deportation; and Judah's last king, eyes gouged out, is carried sightless into exile. Murder, mayhem and mercy – it's all there!

Insight

What are we to make of biblical history?
Despite the recurring features common to human nature, biblical history is essentially linear – moving from past through present to future; rather than, as in some ancient cultures, cyclical, going round and round in an unbreak-able cycle of repetition and fate. More than linear, it would be better to say that biblical history is teleological and theological. Teleological in having a beginning, a middle and an end, it is history which is not random and mean-ingless but history that is going some-where. Even the annual festivals of harvest which follow the rhythm of the seasons were expropriated by Israel for telling the larger story of Israel's

> **Murder, mayhem and mercy – it's all there!**

Insight

partnership with a God who is both Creator and Saviour. This history is theological because the "going somewhere" ultimately has to do with the story God is telling in Scripture. Human characters and events become significant for biblical historians because of their relationship to what God is doing in working out His purposes through human history. Biblical history is essentially redemptive history, tracing the course of God's promise to bless Abraham and the nations as it makes its uncertain way through Israel's own history.

We will miss the message of the biblical history books if we insist on treating them as an objective, factual, reporting of events – this is to seek to make ancient "history" conform to modern, post-Enlightenment demands. In fact, it's now universally accepted that no such purely "objective" history exists. All history is told from some standpoint, urging some point of view. This doesn't make it untrue, rather it is a different kind of truth, one which is less interested in a kind of historical archaeology of past events and more interested in their significance and meaning – in this case in their theological meaning and significance.

> **Biblical history is essentially redemptive history.**

Biblical history is "prophetic" history. As Langmead Casserley said many years ago, "the function of a prophet is to interpret to the chosen people the ways of God in history and to discern and proclaim the revelation of the divine purpose in terms of the judgment and mercy of God". This helps to explain why the Jewish canon lists the whole history from Joshua through to 2 Chronicles as "the former prophets".

In the historical narratives, comments John Mackay, the "kings are judged by prophetic standards, so that we are not handling secular history but the story of a people called by God to build his kingdom and reflect his glory on earth". And as Martin Woudstras points out, "ordinary history may highlight natural causes and enlarge upon subjective motives. Not so with biblical historiography. It is essentially prophetic in character."

With this in mind we can now begin to appreciate why the long historical narratives of the Bible, the Books of Kings and Chronicles, cover roughly the same time frame in the story they tell but tell that story rather differently. Each of these dual works selects from their common story those events that emphasise the particular message they are each trying to make. Both works are written from different vantage points and seek to answer different questions. As we shall see, 1 and 2 Kings is written at the time of the exile to Babylon and seeks to explain, by going back over the long history of Israel, why Israel has arrived in exile. 1 and 2 Chronicles goes back over much the same ground but from the point of view at the end of the exile, when the question is much more about the future.

Kings

1 and 2 Kings can largely be seen as the story of how kingship interacted with the prophets God sent to Israel. It is fascinating to note that the prophets were often court officials or were habitually invading the king's space with the word of God. Elijah exemplifies this (1 Kings 17–19) as does Elisha (2 Kings 1–3) and Isaiah (2 Kings 19:1–7, 20–34), together with the lesser lights – Ahijah (1 Kings 11:29), Shemaiah (1 Kings 12:22–24), Micaiah (1 Kings 22:5–28), and the major female prophet, Huldah (2 Kings 22:14–20).

Here we read the tragic story of the covenant unfaithfulness that has brought kings and people to exile in Babylon. Covenant faithfulness is the yardstick by which the kings of Israel and Judah are measured. For example, Omri is a powerful ruler in the Northern Kingdom of Israel but his long, 12-year reign, is passed over in six verses because "he did evil in God's sight" (1 Kings 16:23–28). On the other hand, Josiah is highlighted because he instituted covenant renewal during his reign (2 Kings 22–23). Notable deviations from adherence to the covenant receive extended attention when especially involving strong prophetic critique. For example, Ahab and Elijah (1 Kings 17).

1 and 2 Kings is not all negative reflection. It depicts disloyalty to the Mosaic covenant as decisive for the waning of Israel's fortunes. But it also consistently emphasises the significance of the Davidic covenant for the nation's destiny and ongoing hope. God's crucial promise to David is "a lamp that will not go out" even as the storm clouds gather over the nation (1 Kings 11:36; 15:4; 2 Kings 8:19). Even at the terrible division of the kingdoms God is merciful because of David (1 Kings 11:12–13, 32). David remains the somewhat idealised standard of kingship throughout (1 Kings 9:4; 11:4 etc.). These almost incidental references in historical narrative are in fact the key moments of theological summary which either seal the fate of, or offer a glimmer of hope to the people of God.

> **Covenant faithfulness is the yardstick by which the kings of Israel and Judah are measured.**

1 and 2 Kings therefore highlight the role of God's prophetic word in shaping history, with internal promise-

fulfilment connections made in the text. For example,
2 Samuel 7:13 is picked up in 1 Kings 8:20; 1 Kings
11:29–32 and 12:15; 13:2 and 2 Kings 23:16. The "former
prophets" contain a "history of the prophetic word" (Peter
Craigie). 1 and 2 Kings is a retrospective evaluation of
Israel's story, explaining that the exile had befallen God's
people, just as Deuteronomy had warned, because both
people and kings had broken the covenant, and offering
the perpetuation of the Davidic promises as the only
gleam of hope for the future.

Chronicles

1 and 2 Chronicles was written after the Exile to bolster
the morale of the restored community devastated by it
and sobered, perhaps, by the penetrating analysis made
in 1 and 2 Kings. The Chronicles' writer too is concerned
to present Israel's history in a certain light and for a particular purpose. In reviewing the story of the Davidic
kingship, the Chronicler adds material and omits material
to suit his particular purpose. For example, the changes
he makes to the account of the Davidic promise given in
2 Samuel 7:1–17 show how he is re-interpreting the
history to make his own special point. The Chronicles'
writer's aim, apparently, was not to re-write or replace the
account in Samuel and Kings but to offer a different viewpoint. He omits the Samuel reference (2 Sam. 7:13) to the
chastisement of David's descendants, preferring, it seems,
to highlight Solomon's obedience.

Since at the time of writing the Davidic kingdom had
crumbled into exile, he changes the phrase "your house
and your kingdom shall endure for ever before me" (2
Sam. 7:16) to "I will set him over my house and my
kingdom for ever" (1 Chron. 17:14). His intention seems
to be to evoke the possibility that though "Israel no
longer has a human king on the throne, the Davidic line

Insight

has not vanished and neither has God's promise, which after all was made personally to David" (Philip Long, *The Art of Biblical History*, Zondervan, pp.82–4 – very helpful for understanding the historical books).

For the people now back in the Land, the question is not the one asked by Kings, "Why has this exile happened to us?", but the one now implicitly asked and answered by the Chronicles' writer: "Are the covenants still in force? Is there hope for us after exile? Do we have a future with this covenant God?" To achieve this – and perhaps to stimulate the rebuilding of the Temple – the Chronicles' writer takes time and trouble to describe the original Temple building in great detail. No doubt in conjunction with this intention went the emergence of the Psalm collection, long held to originate with David, so that the compilation of the Psalter became the lasting Davidic legacy to the post-Exilic community.

The writer underlines his intentions by his repeated emphasis on the sovereignty of God in choosing David (1 Chron. 28:4), Solomon (28:5–6), Jerusalem (2 Chron. 6:6) and the Temple itself (2 Chron. 7:12) where He has entrusted His Name! The changes we have noted to the account of the Davidic covenant (1 Chron. 17 cf. 2 Sam. 7) and the idealised portraits of David, Solomon, Asa, Jehoshaphat, Hezekiah and Josiah, both make the same point. It's as if to say God can wipe the slate clean for you too! And the continual reminders of the Davidic covenant are Messianic markers pointing to the ideal king to come.

Another important point to note is that the Chronicles' writer keeps all Israel in view, both north and south, evidently considering the restored post-Exilic community as a remnant of all Israel. He does this by recounting

how, after the Northern kingdom fell, Hezekiah invited
many from the north to come south to celebrate Passover,
and that some of them stayed (2 Chron. 30; 31:6) to be
present later at Josiah's Passover (2 Chron. 34:9;
35:17–18).

The Chronicles' writer ends on a note of prophetic
fulfilment both in the judgment of exile and the hope of
return (2 Chron. 36:16; 36:21–22 cf. Jer. 25:11; 29:10). So
we can summarise by saying, in Bill Dumbrell's words, that
Kings and Chronicles are "prophetic works, a theological
interpretation which displays a sense of what was ultimately important for the history of the people of God."

Solomon

Solomon is known for his wisdom and yet in his old age he became one of the most foolish people that have ever lived. If we can understand the same influences in our own lives that turned his heart to foolishness, we can be even wiser than Solomon!

It is never enough just to begin a race well, like the hare that stormed ahead but was eventually distracted and stopped running. It is better to be like the slow but determined tortoise who kept going to actually cross the finishing line. Solomon began his walk with God well, creating a magnificent temple, dispensing judgments of great wisdom and writing proverbs of astute understanding. He suppressed Israel's enemies and brought peace and immense wealth to his country. The nation became so rich that even silver lost its value because of the vast reserves of gold (1 Kings 10:14–29). The Bible warns us, however, to be careful when we become wealthy because then we begin to trust and rely on our own resources rather than upon God (Ps. 62:10; Prov. 30:8).

Solomon wrote the book of Ecclesiastes to describe his quest for personal fulfilment. Here he explains how he sought satisfaction by inaugurating a great public works programme, compiling valuable collections, organising sensational orchestras, arranging sumptuous banquets, pursuing educational research and even building a harem with seven hundred wives and three hundred concubines (Eccles. 2). Solomon eventually confesses that all of his activities were a vain "chasing the wind" and that true fulfilment could only be found in a close relationship with God.

It was Solomon's unbridled pursuit of fulfilment that was his undoing. About six hundred years previously Moses had written God's instructions explaining that the Israelites should not compromise their faith by marrying people from other nations who worshipped other gods (Exod. 34:12–17). This was not God demonstrating racism and it was not a totally exclusive ban because Boaz married the converted Moabite, Ruth, who became the ancestor of King David and even Jesus Himself.

In simple terms God was explaining that when we have a very close relationship with people of another belief, it can damage our own and lead us into harmful and sinful practices. 1 Kings 11:1–11 records that Solomon ignored this commandment not only by marrying women of other faiths, but also building temples for their foreign gods, Chemosh and Molech, on the Mount of Olives. (One aspect of worshipping Molech was ritual child abuse and sacrifice by fire (Lev. 18:21; 2 Kings 23:10).) Even though God appeared twice to Solomon, he refused to follow the Lord's commands and even began to worship the foreign gods himself, resulting in the eventual destruction of his kingdom.

There is none so foolish as one who has known wisdom and deliberately chooses to ignore it. Solomon the wise became Solomon the fool. He eventually thought his own wisdom superior to the wisdom of God clearly expressed in the commandments. Solomon thought he could ignore them and find fulfilment but instead he found futility and destruction.

How similar is the message written by Paul over one thousand years later in the book of Romans: "Claiming

themselves to be wise without God, they became utter fools instead" (Rom. 1:22 TLB). How similar too, is our modern technological world in its haste to abandon the eternal truths of God's Word for our own unbridled pursuit of fulfilment and the "wisdom" of modern man, often summed up in the phrase, "if it feels good, do it". This creed instead demonstrates the foolishness of modern man, for the fruit seemed good to Adam and beautiful women seemed good to Solomon, but both led to their destruction, just as rejecting God's wisdom expressed through His Word could lead to our own downfall. Let us seek to finish our own race of faith and become even wiser than Solomon by continually learning and constantly obeying the only true everlasting wisdom – God's Word.

Psalms

FORUM VOICE
Having read Psalm 55:13–14 I am unsure who David was referring to here. He talked about a man of his equal, could this possibly be Ahithophel, King David's counsellor in 2 Samuel 15:12 (who is also Bathsheba's grandfather)?

COVER TO COVER RESPONDS
Bible scholars consider that it is Ahithophel that David is referring to and he is actually named in the Chaldee language paraphrase. Ahithophel was very highly regarded – see 2 Samuel 16:23. It is also prophetic of Judas's betrayal of Jesus. A number of Bible scholars believe that some of the Psalms are prophetic and even the Jewish Rabbis regarded several as "Messianic". That is, they were prophetic of the Messiah who was to come, although they were looking to a conquering saviour, not a suffering one. Some New Testament passages directly quote the Psalms and apply them to Jesus (for example: Psalm 69:9 and John 2:17; Psalm 41:9 and John 13:18; Psalm 22:18 and John 19:24; Psalm 34:20 and John 19:36; and Psalm 68:18 and Ephesians 4:8).

FORUM VOICE
I think the following provides a great variation on the 23rd Psalm for modern life:

The Lord is my pacesetter, I shall not rush during the day.
He makes me stop for quiet intervals, to plan my life.
He provides me with images of stillness, which restore my serenity in the rush.
He leads me in ways of efficiency through calmness of mind in doing tasks wisely. And His guidance is peace in choosing the proper tasks.
Even though I have many things to accomplish each day, I will not fret, for His presence is here.
His timelessness, His all-importance will keep me in balance.
He prepares refreshment and renewal in the midst of my activity with quiet time.

By anointing my mind with His oils of tranquillity.
My cup of joyous energy overflows as I charge ahead!
Surely, harmony and reflectiveness shall be the fruit of my hours,
For I shall walk in the path of my Lord and dwell in His house forever.

COVER TO COVER RESPONDS
This is actually based on a Japanese version compiled by Toki Miyashina and originally broadcast from London by Rev. Eric Frost on 4 May 1965. It emphasises the great adaptability of the Psalms to us as individuals today. There is also a mountaineer's version, a schoolgirl's version and even a version for the space age which begins "The Lord is my Controller, I shall not deviate. He places me in true orbit around my planet Earth. He plotteth my course across the vacuum of space. He directs me safely through the maze of stars." Why not compose your own version to reflect your experience? You can have some fun with this – here's another version:

The Lord is my programmer, I shall not crash
He installed His software on the hard disk of my heart
All of His commands are user-friendly
His directory guides me to the right choices for His name's sake
Even though I scroll through the problems of life I will fear no bugs, for He is my backup
His password protects me
He prepares a menu before me in the presence of my enemies
His help is only a keystroke away
Surely goodness and mercy will follow me all the days of my life
and my file will be merged with His and saved forever

Now it's your turn!

FORUM VOICE
Here's my Psalm:

O Father I declare Your awe to you, my Lord and Saviour,
I will give for evermore my praise and thanks.
You understand our weakest parts,
Forgive us when we've fallen;
So we respond with faithful hearts
In never-ending praise.
O Lord of all creation
Your words are our commands
And in our meditation we share our love for You.
Our heavenly Father grant us, when we see the needs of others,
In faithful love, compassion, then Your comfort to bring.
My Father, I will sing in praise of Your sweet, holy name
My heart will be through all my days
Filled with love for You.

Biblical Symbolism

ForumVoice

FORUM VOICE

I am very interested in the biblical meanings of colours and numbers. (For example, the number four often appears in relation to the "Created Order": Four ends of the earth – North, South, East and West; four seasons; four lunar phases; the four time zones of morning, noon, evening and night; and the four watches of the night.)

COVER TO COVER RESPONDS

Biblical symbolism is a fascinating subject and I can suggest *Numbers in Scripture* by E. Bullinger, published by Bagster, and *The Study of the Types* by A. Habershon, published by Kregel of Grand Rapids, Michigan.

A word of warning is that biblical symbolism should not turn into biblical mysticism, and you need careful discernment because a type can have several and possibly opposite meanings, for example a lion can be Jesus (Rev. 5:5), the devil (1 Pet. 5:8) or an animal (Judg. 14:5).

FORUM VOICE

When we look at the way symbolism is woven into Scripture we see how we serve a God of great detail. Everything is so carefully planned and beautifully made. How small I feel when I think about this awesome Creator.

FORUM VOICE

Your discussion about symbolic meanings got me thinking about another area of symbolic meaning – this is a scripture talking about stones. I would love to hear your opinions on the meanings in this scripture (Isa. 54:11–12 NKJ) "O you afflicted one, tossed with tempest, and not comforted, behold, I will lay your stones with colourful gems, and lay your foundations with sapphires. I will make your pinnacles of rubies, your gates of crystal, and all your walls of precious stones." I would love a deeper understanding of these two verses.

COVER TO COVER RESPONDS

The context of Isaiah 54 is of a widowed, barren woman, a situation which would have been almost a living death. Her widowhood may be due to desertion rather than the death of her husband. In the midst of desertion, rejection, abject shame and poverty God speaks that He will be her husband, she will have many children and great riches. The woman who is despised will be loved and honoured. This is prophetic of Israel and particularly the city of Jerusalem, which will be rebuilt not with just ordinary stones of rock but with precious stones or jewels including sapphire and rubies.

Read Isaiah 54 in the NIV and then read about the new Jerusalem in Revelation 21:9–21. We are also in the position of shame for our sin, spiritually poor and bankrupt, tormented by guilt and unable to be comforted or rescued. Then comes Jesus, not just to save us but to beautify us and make us His bride. What a Salvation! Read also Ezekiel 16:1–14 and then all of Revelation 21 again. In this context then, stones refer to precious jewels and speak of love for the unloved, beauty for ashes, acceptance for rejection, peace for torment and riches for poverty. In particular, precious jewels speak of a wedding and the beauty preparation of the bride.

In another context, stones still refers to precious jewels but they are related to the stones on the breastplate of the High Priest (Exod. 28:15–30). Each of the 12 stones was engraved with the name of one of the tribes of Israel. A number of Bible scholars have linked tribes and stones to suggest symbolism for each stone. For example, a diamond is hard, like the tribe of Gad and can resist attempts to destroy it. We are overcomers in Jesus (1 John 4:4).

FORUM VOICE

What is the symbolic meaning of the hem of a garment/robe if any?

COVER TO COVER RESPONDS

It depends on the garment and who is wearing it. In Matthew 9:20 and Matthew 14:36 just touching the hem or the edge of Jesus' cloak resulted in healing, in the same way in Acts 19:12 handkerchiefs carried the healing power of Paul.

Similarly, in Exodus 28:33–34 and 39:25–26 the hem of the High Priest's robe had miniature bells and pomegranates, speaking of good news and fruitfulness.

The hems of Jewish garments often had tassels, which were permanent reminders of God and His Word to prevent us from walking into sin (see Num. 15:37–41). Similarly in Exodus 13:9,16 and Deuteronomy 6:8, 11:18, the Israelites were commanded to bind portions of the law to their clothes. These became the phylacteries, which the Pharisees ostentatiously wore in the times of Jesus (see Matt. 23:5).

On Reflection

- How can you apply the lesson from Solomon into your own life situations?

- Do you need to seek forgiveness and reconciliation with anyone where there has been a quarrel?

- Do you feel able, like David in the Psalms, to express negative emotions to God?

- There were roles for many people in the Temple. What is your role in the church?

- Why is unity so important? What can you do to improve unity in your church?

- Could using Solomon's prayer as a model help your own prayer life?

- Are there any "little foxes" that are attacking your vine relationship with the Lord?

- Do you tend towards prayer or gossip when you hear about people in difficulties?

- Are there any issues in your life where you need to trust in the Lord and not rely on your own understanding?

- Where do you fall on a scale between laziness and diligence?

CommentOn   *Cover to Cover* Forum

http://www.cover2cover.org/docs/forhome.htm

6

Window on Isaiah

By any account Isaiah of Jerusalem was a remarkable
man. His prophetic ministry spanned the 60 year reign
of four Judean kings (Uzziah, Jotham, Ahaz, Hezekiah)
during the second half of the eighth century BC.
Apparently able to move easily in court circles, Isaiah
spoke the Word of God to kings and nations in a critical
phase of the history of God's people. He lived through
the nerve-jangling Assyrian threat to Judah and felt the
pain of the demise of the Northern Kingdom of Israel
when Samaria fell to the invaders in 722 BC. Married to
a prophetess by whom he had symbolically named sons,
Isaiah, like all true prophets of God, not only spoke, but
to some extent embodied, God's message in his own
experience (Isa. 6:1) and behaviour (Isa. 20:1).

The book that bears his name is majestic in scope and
magnificent in content. It seems to gather up all the
richness of previous Old Testament revelation and project
it forward in fruitful ways into the New Testament era.
In its theology and structure it virtually encapsulates the
whole of the Bible. In the words of current evangelical
commentator John Oswalt, "If the book is read in its
wholeness today, it will continue to unite the two
Testaments as no other book can." The particular fascina-
tion of the book of Isaiah arises from the fact that it
seems to have three distinct strands:

• Chapters 1–39 relate to the crisis posed by Assyrian
imperial expansion from 750 BC onwards. This destroyed
the Israel of the Divided Kingdom and its capital Samaria
in 722 BC and later, around 701, ravaged Judah and
threatened to engulf Jerusalem "up to its very neck" (8:8).

Chapters 36–39 form the bridge linking this crisis, which

Insight

Judah will survive (36–37), to the future invasion by the Babylonians, which it will not (38–39). In the extended period of danger, Isaiah urged first Ahaz (7–9) and later Hezekiah (36–39) to put their entire trust in God rather than unreliable political alliances with foreign powers. With the future of the failed monarchy increasingly in doubt, Isaiah begins to lay clues for an ideal king to come (7, 9, 33).

• Chapters 40–55 offer comfort and hope in stunning visions of salvation and new creation. It makes best sense read as addressed to the traumatised exiles in Babylon, reeling from the destruction of Jerusalem in 585 BC and the loss of kingship, temple, and land. Isaiah brings good news of God's strange work of judgment and even stranger means of grace in raising up the pagan Medo-Persian Emperor, Cyrus, as his "anointed" deliverer of His people (45:1). Cyrus will conquer the Babylonians and decree the release of God's people and return to the Land.

"Isaiah sums up biblical theology in a better way than does any other single book of the Bible" (John Oswalt).

Beyond this Isaiah projects the appearance of a mysterious Suffering Servant – one who will fulfil the vocation of a failed Israel by being the true Israelite, God's faithful covenant partner, prepared to restore the people to their holiness and covenant destiny.

• Chapters 56–66 seem to reflect the post-Exilic situation where returning exiles struggle to rebuild their ruined city and shattered Temple and seek to regain their identity as God's people. Tension still seems to persist between the "righteous" and the compromisers as Isaiah probes the ambiguous response of the people to the renewed call to spiritual worship and social justice.

This enigma remains unresolved. The earlier critical consensus which explained this by posing three distinct authors has broken down under the renewed weight of scholarly attention given to the undoubted overall unity of the book. But no doubt remains about the power and significance of the sweeping prophetic panorama. The theological unity of Isaiah is impressive. "Isaiah sums up biblical theology in a better way than does any other single book of the Bible" (John Oswalt).

It takes faith to be a servant people and a servant king, as the contrast between Ahaz (6–8) and Hezekiah (36–39) reveals. Isaiah chapters 1–39 have been termed a "critique of dominant ideology" (Walter Brueggemann). Political events on the world stage are shaking the foundations of the false security of the Israelite and Judean kings, exposing the misplaced faith of king and people in human pride and power, all at the expense of that risky trust in God which makes possible the vulnerable role of servanthood.

Isaiah (1–39 and 40–66) mirrors the painful reversion from earthly kingship to divine kingship, shown by the arrangement of the Psalms (Pss. 72–89 and 90). God is "the Holy One of Israel", the one Creator and Lord of Creation and therefore the one Redeemer of His people and His world (40–49). Isaiah was the first to strike the "apostolic" note that "God took the responsibility of creating the world because he knew He possessed the power to redeem and retrieve whatever creation might come to" (P.T. Forsyth). Isaiah insists that the nation's extremities are God's opportunities. World events are going His way, or as John Goldingay has it, "God is not just someone to protect them from crises; he is someone who brings about crises". The convulsions of history are sovereignty bent to His saving purpose.

Hence the hope for an exiled people revolves around two promised figures. An agent of God, the Persian overlord Cyrus, will effect the return to the Land (40–48). But to bring about a return to the Lord as well as the Land requires that the deeper, harder, problem of Israel's inveterate sin and covenantal unfaithfulness be dealt with. For this, Cyrus is not enough, only through an enigmatic Suffering Servant of God (42–53) will God's people return to Him and come home to salvation and peace.

Not for nothing has Isaiah been called "the evangelical prophet". His whole book, and especially chapters 40–55 form the primary seedbed for New Testament theology. The ministry of Jesus is best seen as the long awaited end of exile, with the announcement of forgiveness and the day of grace. This is confirmed by the way in which Isaiah is plundered by the Evangelists to define the "gospel".

Mark starts the Jesus story with Isaiah's "wilderness herald" who, says the Evangelist, is John the Baptist (Isa. 40:9; Mark 1). Matthew particularly sees Jesus as the Isaianic bearer of the good news of God's kingdom of peace and salvation, the one in whom the reign of God arrives on the earthly scene once more (Isa. 52:7; Matt. 4:14–23; see also 12:17; 13:14).

For Luke Isaiah 61:1–3 is the Manifesto of the Messiah, Jesus – the starting point for understanding all He is and intends to do (Luke 4). John is almost certainly deeply indebted to the Isaianic vision of God's salvation too. His unique emphasis on the "I am's" of Jesus probably derives from Isaiah's stress on the incomparability of God, the great "I am" (Isa. 40–48).

Paul's preaching of "justification by faith" derives from Isaiah's vision of the covenantal faithfulness of God going out in power to save (cf. Isa. 51:1–8 with Rom. 1:16–17). This has important repercussions for our understanding of the gospel. Justification is a word with forensic or legal overtones, but in an Old Testament context where God in the law court of the nations decides for His people against their enemies. It has nothing to do with any "just-as-if-I'd never-sinned" talk.

Justification is not how we become Christians, but the declaration that we are Christians. It represents the fulfilment of Isaianic hope that God will one day act to restore His people to covenant righteousness and relation-ship. To be justified is to be declared a member of the covenant family of God on the basis of faith in Messiah Jesus. All this is rooted in Isaiah, and only Jesus joined together the royal, Messianic hopes of Isaiah and his portrait of the Suffering Servant.

Only after Cross and Resurrection did the pieces fit together and the good news dawn that through the judgment and "death" of exile had come the restoration of Israel and salvation for the world. And still ahead lies the prophetic and apostolic vision – of the new creation "bursting out all over" as "new heavens and new earth" (Isa. 65–66 and Rom. 8; 2 Pet. 3; Rev. 21–22).

BibleLives

Elijah

One of the greatest discoveries we can make in studying
Bible lives is that the people God used were just like us.
They were not spiritual supermen or superwomen but
fallible, weak human beings. It is this revelation that can
personally inspire us that God can use even us today.
Despite my sins, my faults, my weaknesses and my fears
God can so deeply work in my life that I can be an
instrument in His hands. He does not wait until we
become perfect, but like Elijah He works through us even
though we are still imperfect.

Although Elijah appears in the Old Testament, it is in the
New Testament book of James that the weakness of his
humanity is fully revealed. In James 5:17 we read in the
Amplified version, "Elijah was a human being with a
nature such as we have." Elijah lived with feelings, affec-
tions, and a constitution like ours. Heinz Cassier translates
the same Scripture as, "Elijah was a man with the same
frail power as ourselves".

Elijah was a person of flesh and blood, with emotions
ranging from spiritual exhilaration to suicidal depression.
He demonstrated incredible levels of faith but was also
prone to absolute despair. At one moment he faced and
defeated 850 false prophets single-handedly, but then, at
the next moment, he fled in terror at a woman's threat to
kill him (1 Kings 19).

The name Elijah in Hebrew means "Strength of the Lord".
As a human being, Elijah was inclined to volatile

emotions and mood swings, but when he focused on God, Elijah received the strength of the Lord to overcome both his own weaknesses and those who opposed God. James 5:17 goes on to disclose the secret of the power that transformed a feeble person into the "strength of the Lord". It reveals, "Elijah prayed earnestly".

When Elijah prayed for no rain, there was a drought, he prayed again and there was a thunderstorm. He prayed for provision of oil and flour for the widow, prayed to raise her son from the dead and prayed down fire from heaven upon the sacrifice. He fled for his life in a human response to Jezebel's intimidation, but it was when Elijah was in prayerful conversation with God that his depression lifted and he resumed his powerful prophetic ministry.

Notice that Elijah did not just pray, he prayed earnestly. *The Message* paraphrase reads, "Elijah … prayed hard". These were not feeble, dutiful prayers of a person whose mind was occupied with a thousand and one other issues, but someone who passionately cried out to God from the very depths of his heart.

The book of James encourages us with the thought that if Elijah did it, then so can we. We are no different to this feeble man who was filled by the strength of the Lord according to the deep yearning of his prayers. Notice not only Elijah's fervency in prayer but also his persistence. He prayed three times before the dead boy was raised to life (1 Kings 17:21) and seven times before the rain-clouds appeared (1 Kings 18:41–46).

Like Elijah, our whole-hearted persistent prayers can turn our fear to faith, our doubt to certainty, our timidity to boldness and our self-pity to a burning concern for

others. The message of Elijah is not only that he was a human being just like us, but that we can be just like Elijah, demonstrating the "strength of the Lord" that empowers us to the ends of the earth with the message of salvation through faith in Jesus Christ.

Prophet Talk

FORUM VOICE

I love Amos! Such a vibrant and fearless prophet. His answer to Amaziah the priest who reported him to king Jeroboam II was bold. Amaziah got his own prophecy of doom promptly. Unlike Jonah, Amos stood his ground and even with the threat to his life, he refused to run away.

According to Amos, he was neither a prophet nor belonged to the lineage of prophets. He was an ordinary shepherd and a gardener but the Lord called him and made him a prophet. So, were all the prophets in spiritual slumber along with the people of Israel? To me, the lessons here are clear: God could raise up men and women who would be ready to do His work no matter what the prevailing circumstances might be. He raised Gideon, Jehu and others. He also raised David, who was a shepherd boy, to become a warrior, a king, a writer, a musician and a prophet. May God find you and I worthy and ready to be called to service at the needed hour.

FORUM VOICE

As I read the prophetic books, I have come to appreciate and love the prophets who combined inspiration with divine elegance. I am particularly fascinated by Hosea and Isaiah. I love Isaiah. He does not just deliver God's messages, he does so powerfully and eloquently. Consider Isaiah 1:16–19, "Wash you, make you clean; Come now, let us reason together." There are several of such beautiful passages in Isaiah. I hope you are also enjoying the charisma, eloquence and persuasiveness of these lovely but fearless messengers of God. Please catch the fire and power radiated by these prophets whose messages transcend their era.

FORUM VOICE

Hosea 7:8 talks about Ephraim being "a cake not turned". In other words, Ephraim was badly burnt on one side but not properly cooked or baked on the other. The immediate consequences of this are insensitivity, waywardness and suffering. This figurative portrayal by one of our eloquent prophets raises a fundamental question: why was the cake not turned? The prophet gives the answer in verse 6, "their baker sleepeth all the night" (KJV). Who were the bakers? They were the shepherds who would not care for the sheep, prophets who would not want to offend anyone and leaders who would not provide godly leadership.

Apart from the nation of Israel, one can find several examples in Scripture of individual "cakes" that were not turned. Absalom is a good example. We are told that his father never displeased nor rebuked him. Adonijah, Absalom's younger brother was also never chided for anything (1 Kings 1:6) showing that David was generally weak in disciplining his children. While they were hardened externally by pride and ambition, they were rotten inside and all ended their lives abruptly. As a result of these readings I have been moved to check my life whether I am not also a cake not turned. Or am I the baker who sleeps all night? Perhaps we all need to ask ourselves these questions.

On Reflection

- What things of the past may hold us back from experiencing God's promises in the future?

- Do we, like Elijah, need to be more confrontational with the gospel of repentance?

- How can you apply the lesson from Elijah into your own life situations?

- Can you encourage someone to come out of their own cave of despair?

- Are there any seeds of jealousy in your own heart that if left alone may grow into spiritually binding weeds?

- How do you practise being still before God in order to know Him more intimately?

- Is there a servant of God that you can bless in any way?

- How determined are you in seeking more of God and His power?

- Are there any areas of your own temple (life) that need repair?

CommentOn *Cover to Cover* Forum

http://www.cover2cover.org/docs/forhome.htm

7

Kingship

Kingship was anticipated in the Torah as integral to God's long-term purposes. Abraham and Sarah were promised that kings would be among their descendants (Gen. 17:6,16) and provision was made for how kings should govern (Deut. 17:14–20) – though the text here seems to be coloured by a wistful sense of what might have been. The eventual emergence of kingship in Israel was however deeply problematic.

Insight

1 Samuel 8 records that Israel, desperate for relief from the chaos at the end of the time of the Judges (Judg. 21:25; 1 Sam. 8:3), clamoured for a king for the wrong reason and then chose the wrong man. The reason was wrong in that Israel "wanted to be like any other nation" – a direct repudiation of her unique vocation to be unlike any other nation. Their preferred king was wrong because in choosing Saul they opted for someone who was not God's choice. Given Samuel's dire warnings about the perversion of the office by exploitative and self-interested kings, the history of the monarchy in Israel may be seen as "downhill" from this moment on.

Israel's embrace of monarchy coincides with a change in the role of the prophets. As 1 Samuel 9:9 suggests, the arrival of kingship in Israel led to the prophets becoming, in effect, "guardians of the theocracy", continually reminding the kings that they ruled only as stewards of God's own Kingship and remained under the authority and scrutiny of God's Word.

The significance of kingship must not be underestimated. Ancient kings not only represented the kingship of their god (sacral kingship) but in a real sense represented their people. As G.B. Caird puts it, "A king is one whose

actions are such that his subjects are included in the doing of them, and whose calamities are such that his subjects are included in the suffering of them. The king did not merely rule Israel: he was Israel." Because the king embodied the destiny of his people, when he failed to walk covenantally with God, the people were brought under judgment with him.

The representational role of the king is illustrated by two points, one general, the other specific. The fact that in a general way the future of the nation is bound up with the person of the king explains why, after 1 Samuel 8, the story of the Israelites becomes the story of the Israelite kings (1 Sam. 10 to 2 Chron. 36). More specific is an interesting point of detail. When Absalom's rebellion is suppressed, a dispute breaks out between the Northern and Southern tribes as to who will have the privilege of escorting the king back to Jerusalem. This right is claimed by Judah on the basis of kinship but Israel replies: "We have ten shares in the king; and besides, we have a greater claim on ['in'] David than you" (2 Sam. 19:40–20:2). To be part of Israel is to have shares in the king – an incorporative concept which, via a very long route, will eventually illuminate what it means for us to be "in Christ".

> **Because the king embodied the destiny of the people, when he failed to walk covenantally with God, the people were brought under judgment with him.**

This incorporative function built into the notion of kingship was reinforced by the covenant God made with David set out in 2 Samuel 7 (by any reckoning one of the most important chapters in the whole Bible). Israel as a nation had been termed God's "son" (Exod. 4:22–23) – now that special bond was focused in the Davidic king, promised in a special "Father–son" relationship. It is vital, not least for our understanding of the New Testament, to grasp that "son of God" language did not in itself carry connotations of divinity, but was particularly the language of kingship – especially suggesting the unique unity between king and people.

This commitment to the Davidic kings, termed a "covenant" in Psalm 89 for example, channelled from here on the redemptive purposes of God for both Israel and through her for the world. Psalm 2 encapsulates this divine determination to make His anointed King ("Messiah") Lord of the whole world.

Kingship found its most famous expression in David himself. Unfortunately David is trivialised by being over-romanticised by lazy preachers looking for quick spiritual lessons who forget that he built his power-base by running a protection-racket. The Chronicler also can't resist this tendency to "airbrush" David's story. But David is an anti-hero, an unlikely underdog, just like Israel, a fugitive who gathers around him a band of desperados; distressed, in debt and discontented. He is the very embodiment of a tough, resourceful survivor who knows his way around a people who, like him, are refugees and marginalised. Only when his heirs forget this did kingship degenerate into playing the power-game like every other tin-pot ancient monarch (e.g. Rehoboam: 1 Kings 12:1–17).

> **David is an anti-hero, an unlikely underdog, just like Israel, a fugitive who gathers around him a band of desperados; distressed, in debt and discontented!**

Insight

The demise of Judah's last king in the Babylonian exile was marked by a reassertion of the kingship of Yahweh, as the composition of the Book of Psalms indicates in the shift from the end of Psalm 89 to Psalm 90, including the subsequent collection of songs celebrating "The Lord reigns". Yet 2 Samuel 7 anchored the promises to David in an unconditional commitment by Yahweh, so that the persistent failure of the occupants of the office did not put it beyond redemption as a vehicle for Yahweh's saving plans.

The unqualified nature of the Davidic covenant of 2 Samuel 7 shows that "divine grace will surpass, survive and overcome even the sins of the royal ideology and its wielders" so that David became a "powerful sign of God's promise in the ongoing story of God's grace to Israel" (Bruce Birch). So, despite the almost total failure of kingship, or perhaps because of it, hopes arose of an "ideal king", a new "David". These hopes are articulated by the prophets (Isa. 9) especially at the Exile (Jer. 23; Ezek. 34–36). This was supplemented by Isaiah's strong insistence on the "return of God as king in Zion" (Isa. 40:7–9; 52:7) who would bring His kingdom of justice, peace and salvation. This is the seedbed of what Jesus understood as "the gospel". Added to this is Isaiah's vision of a mysterious servant of God who is Israel and ministers to Israel and who in this dual capacity can only be some kind of royal personage, though one who strangely, in an unprecedented way, reigns through suffering (Isa. 52:13–53:12).

Kingship remained the focus for hope and expectation even when the Exile forced a heart-searching reassessment of the history of the people and its kings. 1 and 2 Kings, evaluating the long history at the time of the Exile, asks the question: "How did things come to this? Why have we ended up in exile?" – and found the reason in the royal shepherds who had led God's flock in paths of covenantal unrighteousness. The Chronicler, at the end of Exile, reviews the same historical time-frame but with an eye to the future, asking: "Is there any hope? Especially can any good yet come out of the Davidic dynasty?" His final chapter of 2 Chronicles 36 is open-ended: so the story will go on.

As a category of hope kingship persisted but more as a kind of "watch this space" notice until it began to be "coloured in" beside the Jordan when the heavens parted and the Voice (the Psalmist had heard from the throne in Psalm 2) singled out a man who had emerged from the river with the words "You are my Son". So, whatever else we know about Jesus of Nazareth, we now know He is anointed and designated as Israel's King.

As a result we can say that "just as David represented God to the people of Israel, so Jesus represents God to those who see in His face the glory of the Lord. Just as David was the people of Israel and represents them before God, so Jesus incorporates the people He has come to save" (Caird). That He would be a suffering, servant King was His great enigma, resolved only by His resurrection, which was the occasion when God publicly affirmed His Son's Kingship: "Today I have become your Father!" (Acts 13:33). In such a way, Israel's King, as Psalm 2 had insisted, became Lord of the whole world (Acts 2:36).

> **Just as David represented God to the people of Israel, so Jesus represents God to those who see in His face the glory of the Lord.**

Kingship "filled-full", and redefined by Easter and Pentecost crystallises the challenge we face. The measure of our free and joyful submission to the Lordship of this Servant–Son–King Jesus, will, as before, be the measure of whether we retain our distinctiveness as a "holy nation" or succumb to the temptation to serve lesser lords and become just "like any other people"!

Hezekiah

The life of Hezekiah stands out from the rest of the kings like the full moon stands out from the stars in the night sky. 2 Kings 18:5 says of him, "Hezekiah trusted in the Lord, the God of Israel. There was no-one like him among all the kings of Judah, either before him or after him". The name Hezekiah in Hebrew means "God is my strength" and is partly derived from the root *hhazaq* which is translated as "to hold fast, be strong, be coura-geous". Why was Hezekiah such an outstanding king? The answer is found in 2 Kings 18:6–7, "he followed the Lord in everything, and carefully obeyed all of God's commands to Moses. So the Lord was with him and pros-pered everything he did" (TLB). His ardent desire to worship and obey God transformed the faithless and idol-atrous nation into a people that once again turned their hearts towards the Lord.

There are many renowned episodes from Hezekiah's life that demonstrate his qualities of faith, determination, prayerfulness and encouragement. However, it can be interesting to look at one of his lesser known achieve-ments which is nonetheless full of spiritual teaching.

In the scorching heat and arid landscape of the Middle East water is a very precious commodity. There are very few rivers and so most water was obtained by sinking wells deep into the rock strata where there were vast underground reservoirs. In the Old Testament, wells are a recurring theme, particularly in the lives of the patriarchs such as Abraham, Isaac and Jacob. Where they found

water, there could be life and a thriving community. Where there was no water there would only be death. In some places springs of water would issue from the ground and provide water. Jerusalem was built on a series of hills and did not have its own natural water supply. Just outside the city walls however, the Gihon spring supplied water for its inhabitants. This meant that Jerusalem was particularly vulnerable to attack from its enemies who, by laying siege to the city, could command and cut off the water supply.

Hezekiah was a great builder. He restored the Temple and built fortified cities throughout Judah, but perhaps his greatest engineering project was to safeguard Jerusalem's water supply. We read in 2 Chronicles 32:1–5 that when King Sennacherib of Assyria planned to besiege Jerusalem, Hezekiah organised "a huge work crew to block [the springs] outside the city, and to cut off the brook running through the fields" (TLB). According to 2 Kings 20:20 he then arranged for workmen to dig an underground tunnel from Gihon spring into the city. The waters flowed into Jerusalem where they formed the Pool of Siloam, which is referred to in the New Testament (John 9:7–11).

In 1880 a young boy wading in this pool went into the entrance to the tunnel and found an inscription celebrating the completion of the work dating back to 702 BC. The stone bearing the inscription is now in the Orient Museum in Istanbul, but if you visit Jerusalem today you can actually walk through Hezekiah's tunnel and re-live Bible history.

Water in the Bible represents life and its vital necessity for all living creatures. Water can even transform the searing desert into a luxuriant oasis. Jesus said that those who believed on him would have within them a spring of living water that represented the same Holy Spirit who brought life to the original creation (John 7:37–39). Without the Holy Spirit our faith will be dry and lifeless but with Him our lives will be a fountain of spiritual blessings that will flow out to others.

Hezekiah channelled life-giving water underground to the inhabitants of the earthly Jerusalem, but Jesus channels the life of the Holy Spirit unseen into the hearts of those who belong to the heavenly Jerusalem. Even though we might be surrounded by enemies laying siege to our faith and emotions, we have access to unseen reservoirs of God's vast strength and power. It was that unseen flow of God's life that inspired Hezekiah to initiate revival in an idolatrous nation, gave Daniel courage in the lions' den and caused Paul to praise in prison. In the midst of difficulty we cannot only survive but actually thrive and flourish because God is our strength.

Biblical Humility

FORUM VOICE

I believe the emphasis in God's Word on humility is due to the fact that it helps us to have an uncorrupted heart, which is God's delight. But humility is not an easy thing to get and hold. Someone said humility is something you lose when you think you have it. In other words, you cannot score yourself or mark your own paper when it comes to this important virtue. It cannot be acquired nor kept easily. It has its root in God and one must constantly go to Him for help and assessment. It's a thing of the heart. Christ Himself was humble (Phil. 2:6–9).

Since an uncorrupted heart will always see the Lord, the challenge before me is to ensure that my heart is seriously guarded against the host of things that seek to corrupt it. I am encouraged by Proverbs 23:26 that says I should give God my heart. If I can do this constantly and also ask Him to search my heart regularly there is hope for me.

COVER TO COVER RESPONDS

How might following the principles of Exodus 20:8, Leviticus 23:39–43, Deuteronomy 8:6–18, John 13:1–17 and 1 Corinthians 11:23–26 help us maintain a humble and uncorrupted heart, preventing us repeating the mistakes of the kings?

FORUM VOICE

Thinking particularly about material success, I believe that in biblical times, it was firmly believed that material, or business success was a sign of God's favour, so they assumed that if they prospered, it was because they met with God's approval. This is why it is harder for a rich man to enter the Kingdom than for a camel to pass through the eye of a needle. The rich man thought he was already meeting with God's approval, so giving it up to follow Jesus was not something he could even contemplate. None of us knows what tomorrow brings, but if we are in God's will, it will be for our ultimate good, even if our circumstances change dramatically and in the world's eyes we become poor.

Forum Voice

FORUM VOICE

In times of difficulty many find it easier to seek God in all humility. What I need to worry about is, when all riches have been added unto me, will I still seek God then? Will God have to humiliate me for me to be humble? Will He have to send "Assyria" to plunder me that I may be in line with His will and purposes? (*Cover to Cover*, Day 180). This is my concern.

COVER TO COVER RESPONDS

The key word and concept is "remember". Remember to give God special time, remember our humble origins, remember that we only know God not because of our greatness but because of Christ's death, which we acknowledge by Communion. God specifically gave the Israelites the Festival of Tabernacles (or Tents) so they would vacate their beautiful houses for humble tents, lest they forgot that their wealth was all due to Him. Jesus humbled Himself from the wealth and glory of heaven to become a servant and performed humiliating tasks such as washing His disciples' feet. He is our perfect example.

George Muller decided on a standard of living and any money in excess of this he gave away. Some people operate a "sliding tithe" where they give away 10% on a basic level of income, 20% on the next £10,000, 30% on the next £10,000 and so on. We should not be frightened of possessions or avoid wealth, but perhaps should take steps to avoid its corrupting influence. My wealthy neighbour, who travels the world first class on business, takes a week's holiday to go with sick and dying children to Lourdes. A leader of a successful church cleans the lavatories during a week-long open-air tent mission.

If you are in a position of power or wealth what could you do to avoid the corruption of pride? Although these acts can become rituals they can also be practical ways of ensuring that we avoid pride in our possessions and achievements by remembering that we owe everything to God and are called to perform the most menial tasks for our fellow human beings.

FORUM VOICE

Another way of looking at the lessons on maintaining a humble and uncorrupted heart is exemplified by the principle followed by king Asa in 2 Chronicles 15:8. Following his overwhelming defeat of the Ethiopians who greatly outnumbered him, and the encouraging prophecy of Oded, Asa renewed the altar of the Lord. He also led the whole country in making a covenant with God.

The spiritual atmosphere of the country changed for the better. There is no better way of celebrating victory than bringing the "spoils" accruing from the victory to the Lord and then renewing the altar of the Lord both physically and spiritually as Asa did. I am encouraged to follow this principle regularly, especially in time of success when I am most tempted to be carried away. One should be prepared to pay the cost of renewing the altar of the Lord. It would involve putting away all that constitute dregs or hindrances in our lives. For Asa, the cost was putting away his own mother from being the queen.

On Reflection

- How concerned are you about the spiritual health of future generations and what could you do to help them?

- Are there any religious articles or attitudes you unconsciously worship and need to "put away"?

- How can you apply the lesson from Hezekiah into your own life situations?

- Are there any idols in your life that should be destroyed?

- Are you aware of any hardness in your heart that needs to be broken up to produce fruitful soil?

- What are you and your church sowing and what harvest will it produce?

- When you are in trouble, to what extent do you look to the natural resources of others instead of the supernatural resources of the Lord?

- Have you received bad news that you need to share with God and ask for His help?

- Are you aware of any wounds in your own life that have only been treated superficially and still cause you great pain?

- Do you, like Jeremiah, feel inadequate for the task God has given you. How can God's Word and God's people encourage you?

CommentOn   *Cover to Cover* Forum

http://www.cover2cover.org/docs/forhome.htm

141

8

Jeremiah
– The Passionate Prophet

Jeremiah, who prophesied between 626 BC and 584 BC, wielded the classic two-edged sword of the biblical prophets – judgment and hope. This dual role is perfectly summed up in the Lord's call to "uproot and tear down, to destroy and overthrow, to build and to plant" (Jer. 1:10).

His lengthy and wide-ranging ministry is without parallel in the Old Testament, not least for the loneliness he experienced and the hostility he faced. "His wide spiritual vision combined the fearlessness of Amos, the loving concern of Hosea and the stern grandeur of Isaiah ..." writes R.H. Harrison.

Jeremiah – a man of God's heart
In his call and commission, the word of the Lord came to Jeremiah (Jer. 1:4, 7, 10, 17–19) and became the driving force in his turbulent life. He has been described as "a man to whom God's persistent, inescapable, and overriding Word has been delivered. His life consists of coming to terms with that Word, finding ways to articulate it to his contemporaries, and living with the hazardous consequence of that reality" (Walter Brueggemann).

The word of the Lord became the driving force in his turbulent life.

Jeremiah's relationship with God was deep but painful. The God who had promised to be with him and for him sometimes seems absent, even against him. This tension of transcendence (God being holy and awesome) and immanence (God being intimate and unthreatening) had to be kept unresolved if his prophetic edge was to be maintained (Jer. 23:23).

Insight

Jeremiah's sensitivity is that of a man who feels deeply, a man who wears his heart on his sleeve. He is passionate and free in expressing his emotions, not least directly to God in complaint and lament – a burningly honest way of relating to God reflected in the Psalms. These outbursts of outrage are, not surprisingly, termed Jeremiah's "lamentations". He feels himself dragged along "like a gentle lamb led to the slaughter" (11:18–23). God doesn't exactly overflow with sympathy: "If you have raced with men on foot and they have worn you out, how can you compete with horses?" (12:5). Words of harsh comfort indeed.

In our day we might consider Jeremiah a suitable candidate for inner healing.

The agonised self-confession of chapter 15 (vv. 10–21) sees Jeremiah bemoan his own birth, complaining that his pain is "unending" and his wound "incurable", accusing God of being "a deceptive brook".

Then Jeremiah acknowledges that the heart is "deceitful above all things" and pleads for healing, but he still waxes indignant that the Lord allows him to suffer so much. He even accuses God of so abusing him as to have "deceived" him (Jer. 20:7). This is extreme language but shows us a man who is no plastic prophet, rather one who is totally and emotionally involved in the prophetic role and whose nerve endings are at full stretch in the service of this strange but compelling God.

God's Word is the cause of Jeremiah's trouble but he can't escape it: it rages in him as an unquenchable and uncontainable fire (20:9). Yet God is not only the antagonist but his protagonist, who will be like a "mighty warrior" to him and to whom he "has committed his cause" (20:11–12).

In our day we might consider Jeremiah a suitable candidate for inner healing. But, like Hosea, Jeremiah shows us that a true prophet is not a mechanical conduit for God's Word to pass through, but a person in whom God's Word takes up residence. So Israel's truest prophets prefigured that an even greater and final embodiment of God's Word would drive His message home not by inflicting suffering on others but by enduring suffering Himself.

What Jeremiah is experiencing is in fact the rawness of God which he seeks to articulate. He feels and expresses what the great Rabbinic teacher, Abraham Heschel, called "the pathos of God". When Jeremiah condemns the false prophets who use their position to exploit and manipulate in self-serving ways, he admits that his "heart is broken … I am like a drunken man … because of the Lord and his holy words" (23:9). He is feeling what God is feeling at this misuse of His Word and name. "His condition was a state of suffering in sympathy with the divine pathos" (Heschel).

> **Hated by those in power and disowned even by his own townspeople, Jeremiah had few friends.**

Hated by those in power and disowned even by his own townspeople, Jeremiah had few friends apart from his loyal secretary, Baruch, who in the end went with the prophet into exile in Egypt.

Jeremiah – a lonely voice for God

Living at one of the great turning points of the Ancient Near Eastern world, Jeremiah's ministry spanned the fall and rise of Empire. From the fall of Assyria, with the destruction of Nineveh in 612 BC, through the desperate attempts of Egypt and Assyria to hold on to cruel power, to the rise of the mighty, ruthless Babylonians who crushed the Egyptians at Carchemish in 605 BC, Jeremiah dared to see beneath the surface of things the sovereign hand of Yahweh.

He knew Judah was doomed, not because he read newspapers or simply understood the signs of the times, but because he was privy to God's sovereignty and His plans to judge His people. Jeremiah brought down trouble on his head for his relentless indictment of the nation's leaders, whether kings, rulers or officials, comparing Jehoahaz unfavourably with his godly father, Josiah. Jeremiah pronounced prophetic woes of judgment on the nation's leaders ("shepherds") offering instead a vision of a future "righteous Branch" of David who would "reign wisely" and bring justice to the land. False prophets were vigorously denounced, especially clashing with the servile Hananiah. Jehoiakim was hostile to him and Jeremiah found himself more often than not in prison in an attempt to shut him up.

Jeremiah hardly made himself more popular by communicating God's direct indictment of the city itself: "I am against you, Jerusalem". But it was his mocking attack on the Temple which roused most ire, as Jeremiah taunted the presumptuous sense of inviolability that had grown up around the site as the dwelling place of God. Chapter 7 encapsulates this brilliant and brave assault on those who used the Temple to escape from the reality of God into phoney religion.

Above all, Jeremiah answered the hotly-debated question of what Judah's response should be to the Babylonian threat by advocating surrender. The pro-Egyptian party urged reliance upon alliance with Egypt while others, seemingly more pious, said simply "trust Yahweh". They did this presumably on the basis of positive confession, believing that if they spoke out the words "peace, peace" loudly and often enough there was nothing to worry about.

However, Jeremiah recommends submitting to the Babylonians and is branded a traitor. Yet such are God's mysterious, even scandalous ways, because, somewhat paradoxically, God's sovereign will is precisely to hand His people over judicially to the Babylonians. This will ultimately become His way of salvation for them. The Imperial Babylonian overlord, Nebuchadnezzar, is to be seen merely as God's servant. We may imagine that conflict and hostility are Jeremiah's lot, "against" is almost his middle name – extending down to the level of even his own family.

> **Jeremiah speaks with poetic passion and stunning imagination**

Jeremiah announces judgment on Israel

Jeremiah is, in Brueggemann's words, a "prophet who speaks with poetic passion and stunning imagination" of judgment and hope. He paints an alternative scenario to the status quo and destruction. He is called to shatter old worlds, to reshape people's perception of reality. To do this, Jeremiah uses powerful images and pictures to subvert current ideas and ideology, exposing lies and all who are deceitful, like Jacob.

Insight

Jeremiah:
- Re-assesses Judah's life against the Mosaic covenant proclaiming judgment, like Hosea, in the vivid metaphor of marriage and adultery
- Describes the shocking effects of God's judgment through war and invasion in the dramatic language of de-creation, as if the reverse button on creation has been pressed and all created things revert to chaos
- Denounces Judah's rationalisations, exposing five false assumptions: "how can you say ...?"
- Portrays Israel's plight as severe wounding which needs healing but wonders whether healing is to be found – "is there no balm in Gilead?"

Jeremiah offers hope for the future

What seemed a disproportionately minor part of his call to be a prophet, that of "building up and planting", eventually surfaces as the long crisis draws to its close. This occurs most notably in the so-called "Book of Comfort or Consolation" (in chapters 30–33) which offers promises of restoration after disciplinary, but not terminal, judgment. Spurred by his covenant-loving kindness, God pledges a remarkable and revolutionary renewal of the covenant relationship. God promises to create a people beyond the "death" of exile who will be changed from the "inside-out".

> **God pledges a remarkable and revolutionary renewal of the covenant relationship.**

God will write His law in their hearts giving them inner direction to do His will. He will re-establish the covenant bond between Him and His people and extend the personal knowledge of Himself across all levels of

society. All of this involves a radical forgiveness of His people's sins – unprecedented in its scope and seemingly independent of the old sacrificial system. A further seven oracles of promise flow from this. Then the prophet makes his contribution to the picture of a new kingship, one that is both Davidic and priestly, which would fulfil the age-old covenant promise made to Abraham (compare Jer. 33:14–22 with Jer. 4:2 and Gen. 12:3).

Jeremiah's identification with Israel
Jeremiah:
- Identifies with Israel in her affliction and anguish (8:18–9:1).
- Identifies with Israel in her affliction by praying for intercession (14:7–9, 19–22).
- Identifies with Israel by embodying her vocation in a remnant of one – demonstrating extraordinary covenant obedience and courage

"His vocation was to incarnate the response to God which all Israel was supposed to make. He had to be willing to be a minority of one" (John Goldingay).

Jeremiah's identification with God
- Jeremiah is overwhelmingly God's man, highlighting that God's truth is not related to our self-generated viewpoint but God's Word.
- Jeremiah speaks with poetic passion and stunning imagination, giving God's truth not in prose but in poetry thus allowing for God's freedom.
- Jeremiah is profoundly engaged in public events, showing us that God's truth is not a private, domestic or devotional matter but impacts public events and political power structures.
- Jeremiah is a man of passionate indignation and conflict, which teaches us that God's truth is not

without dispute in a world unwilling to be disturbed by too much reality and unable to embrace either true joy or deep grief.

Insight

Walter Brueggemann summarises superbly the powerful blend of darkness and light, judgment and grace in Jeremiah's message and ministry when he writes, "Jeremiah's word spoken and envisioned in Israel covered the end of the known world. That world is presided over by the kings and priests of this age, who imagine themselves secure, stable and safe. Jeremiah asserts that the world which is organised against God's covenantal faithfulness, will and must end by the hand of Babylon. If this judgment seems 'too hard' or 'impossible' for Yahweh, He will do it! (32:27)."

At the same time, Jeremiah's word among Judah's exiles is about the beginning of a new world wrought only by the mercy and freedom of God. This is a new possibility, judged by hopeless former rulers to be impossible. They believe there can be no new thing. Such a world with a new David (23:5–6), a new covenant (31:31–34), a new healing (30:17) is always thought to be "too hard" or "impossible" for Yahweh, but Yahweh can do it (32:17). Life begins again when Yahweh is known to be the giver of newness

Jeremiah, as the person who suffers and hopes most in ancient Israel, continues as a powerful presence in the New Testament. The suffering of Jeremiah and the end of Israel which he embodies, the hope of Judah and the new Israel which he articulates, have become models for understanding Jesus, the one who can be destroyed and raised up.

Daniel

Daniel's life was subject to violent disruption and tremendous change, yet he was one of the most stable and composed of Bible characters. Although Daniel operated in the fiercely competitive and corruptible political arena, even his enemies admitted that he was totally trustworthy and he was neither corrupt nor negligent in any of his duties (Daniel 6:4).

When still a young man and living in Jerusalem as a member of the nobility, he was captured by Nebuchadnezzar and forcibly deported 500 miles to Babylon where he had to adapt to a foreign language and culture. Years later when Daniel had risen to a position of high esteem and authority, Darius the Mede conquered the Babylonian empire and Daniel once again confronted the insecurity of enforced change. Throughout all of these upheavals and many other challenges however there was one thing that never changed – Daniel's dedication to God and his determination to obey His commands.

There are several aspects of Daniel's character that are quite remarkable, but perhaps above all else he is noted as an outstanding man of prayer. It was Daniel's prayers that energised his spiritual life to give him supernatural wisdom to interpret visions and administer a vast kingdom (Dan. 2:18; 10:12). He faced every situation with an extraordinary confidence and faith in God, even when he was thrown into the lions' den. In the Bible we are given a number of insights into different elements of

Daniel's prayers that can help us in our own desire to build an effective prayer life.

Even though Daniel was naturally intelligent and quick-witted he realised that only God could provide the wisdom he needed in various situations. He relied not only on his own prayers but he was sufficiently humble to ask others to pray for him (Dan. 2:16–19). In modern parlance, we might say he had prayer partners.

In Daniel 6 we read the story of other jealous administrators trying to trap and remove him from high office. Their one focus is Daniel's prayer life and they trick king Darius into signing a law which decrees that for thirty days any person caught praying to anyone other than the king should be thrown into the lions' den. It is in this story that we learn that Daniel prayed regularly every day, he prayed often, three times a day and that he prayed faithfully and publicly, despite opposition, even if it was to mean his death (Dan. 6:10).

In chapter 9 we find Daniel reading the Scripture in the book of Jeremiah, inspiring him to pray. The intensity of his prayers is astonishing because he clothes himself in sackcloth and covers himself in ashes as a public demonstration to God of his sincere repentance. He fasts and passionately pleads with God for mercy for his nation. In a wonderful example of an intercessor, the righteous and faithful Daniel identifies with his people when he confesses "we have sinned"; "we have been wicked"; "we have not obeyed"; "our unfaithfulness" (Dan. 9:4–20).

Later in Daniel 10:2–3 it records his three-weeks' persistence in prayer and fasting and continual seeking of God until an answer is given. Despite Daniel's immense reputation for wisdom we learn that he did not become proud and arrogant but continued to humble himself in prayer before the Lord (Dan. 10:12).

The New Testament book of James reveals that often we do not receive from God because we do not pray correctly (Jam. 4:2–3). If we would only study and apply the principles of Daniel's prayer life to our own, we too could become a person known for their wisdom and faith in a powerful God. Our intercession for others could lead to their salvation and a mighty move of God in our own nation. It is never enough to just study the lives of Bible characters, we also need to learn and apply the lessons to our own lives that we might be similar instruments of God's purpose for our own land and time.

Daniel

FORUM VOICE

The book of Daniel makes interesting reading. I believe that chapter 3 has a lot of meaning and application for today. The faith of Shadrach, Meshach and Abednego is very challenging. How would you or I have reacted to such a challenge to our faith and allegiance to God? Would we have said "well, everybody is doing it, I am not the only Christian challenged by the decree of the king"? Some others might have said, "it is better to be wise and to avoid direct confrontation with the king".

Some Christians might remind themselves, and others, that God has asked us to obey authorities because they have been set up by God Himself. Finding a biblical quotation for that would have been quite easy since Jeremiah had made several references emphasising the fact that Nebuchadnezzar was God's servant, appointed to subdue nations and that people should serve him. But these three men stood up in faith and refused to bow, even if God would not deliver them. Note that they were actually officers of the king and might have signed an oath of allegiance to him. Yet they chose to honour God above all.

I am also challenged by their unity. What if one or two of them had backed down when faced with the life or death threat of the great king? Isn't it wonderful that they stood their ground and that God honoured their faith? The only things they lost were their chains. God was greatly honoured and His name gained prominence.

Today, we are faced with many golden images to which we must either bow or stand up against like these outstanding men. Unfortunately, these modern images are also "golden" and very often their beauty and attraction obliterate the fact that they are still idols which we must refuse to serve.

Ezekiel

FORUM VOICE

It is obvious that God talks with Ezekiel a lot through visions. Ezekiel was also used as "a sign unto Israel", so he is asked do some strange things to convey the messages graphically to the people. Who says God is not a dramatist? This book shows that He actually founded the ministry of holy Christian drama.

The most important thing that has caught my attention in Ezekiel is that after God might have given him the visions, he would ask him to go ahead and prophesy! Why prophesy again? Is God's Word not immutable? This has now taught me a valuable lesson. We may have dreams and visions from God, but we need to go ahead and prophesy them into existence. Do you remember that after God promised that David's royal line will continue forever through his children, David still went ahead to pray that God would indeed bring it to pass? That was quite good. Maybe he should have gone ahead to prophesy that all his children would know and follow the Lord from their youth to old age. Perhaps that could have averted the tragedy started by Solomon.

I also notice that Ezekiel is not only asked to prophesy good things, like prophesying to dry bones to come alive, but to also prophesy the doom of the wicked and the enemy. So this should add pep to our prayer life. Using God's Word, prophesy that the kingdom and the will of God will come to pass in your life and in the life of nations. God was eager to bring about things quickly in the time of Ezekiel. He is even more eager now to bring His kingdom into lives and the nations of the world.

COVER TO COVER RESPONDS

This is an important principle, as it seems that often when God speaks of the future it is our prayers that will cause that future to happen or not happen. For example, in Ezekiel 36:22–38 God will bless Israel in about 25 different ways, including cleansing them, bringing them into their own land, giving them a new heart and spirit. However, apparently God will not act until Israel pleads with Him to do it. Similarly, in the book of Jonah the

prophecy of the destruction of Nineveh did not take place because the inhabitants prayed and repented before God to spare them. What a privilege and a responsibility we have in prayer that we can work with God as He seeks to bless and challenge His world. We cannot simply sit back with an attitude that God will work no matter what we do, for He has chosen to often limit His own work in direct relationship to our prayers. WOW! Let's get praying!

FORUM VOICE

Thanks for the insight into the link between prophesying and prayer. As I read the Prophets, especially Ezekiel and Jeremiah, it seems to me that there are passages which are not only speaking to God's people of those times, but which are also prophesying things still to be fulfilled in our day. I am not always sure which is which, or whether some passages are speaking to both situations.

On Reflection

- Do you face a situation where you need God's wisdom?

- Take time to look away from your problems and worship God by focusing on His greatness.

- What are you doing with God's gifts to you?

- How much do you rely on your own resources instead of God?

- What is your attitude when God appears to discipline or prune you?

- How can you experience God's love every morning?

- How much of your prayer life is spent asking God's approval of your own plans instead of asking about His plans?

- In what way might we be influenced to worship false gods today?

- What spiritual resolutions could you make?

- How can you apply the lesson from Daniel into your own life situation?

OnReflection

CommentOn   *Cover to Cover* Forum

http://www.cover2cover.org/docs/forhome.htm

9

Insight
Exile and Restoration

Bible Lives
Esther

Forum Voice

On Reflection

Exile and Restoration

The exile of Judah to Babylon, which began around 606
BC and was sealed by the destruction of Jerusalem in 587
BC, was traumatic in the extreme. The basic human pain
of invasion, killing, defeat, and deportation were severe
enough. But the larger implications were no less acute.
In humiliating fashion, "all the tangible marks of empirical
Israel vanished" (Bill Dumbrell).

The deep-seated belief in the absolute security of Israel's
position and the "inviolability of Zion", had been ruthlessly
exposed. The withdrawal of Yahweh's
presence culminated in the heart-
breaking news that the Temple in
Jerusalem had been destroyed. This
seemed the end of Israel's distinctive
identity as the people of this God, and
perhaps even spelled the death of God
Himself! The loss of the Land was felt
most keenly; so long ago it was
promised to the patriarchs and so
dearly won. To lose the Land –
regarded as a "spiritual index of Israel's
political health" (Dumbrell) – was to
fall under the ultimate curse laid on
covenant unfaithfulness by the
Deuteronomic charter (Deut. 28:63;
29:27–28).

> **The withdrawal
> of Yahweh's
> presence
> seemed the
> end of Israel's
> distinctive
> identity as the
> people of
> this God.**

The whole Old Testament story of Israel revolves around
Exodus and Exile. From Exodus – slavery in Egypt, to
Exile – slavery in Babylon. To come from slavery and to
end up in slavery was painful and ironic, all the more so
since Babylonia was where Abraham had come from over

a millennium before. The initial reaction was an intense outpouring of grief.

The exiles "hung their harps on the willow trees", unable to sing the Lord's song in a strange land, even when urged to do so by their mocking captors (Psalm 137). The hurt caused by exile is compressed into the aptly-named Book of Lamentations. It has been described as the most tear-stained book in the whole Old Testament, and for good reason. "Judah has gone into exile … and there is no one to comfort". This refrain is repeated again and again in the opening chapter, as if the writer is stuck in a deep groove of paralysis and pain.

Jeremiah's message touched several stages. Controversially, he began by advocating that people submit to the Babylonian invasion because he read it (correctly) as the judgment of God on His people. Later, writing to the exiles in Babylon, Jeremiah urged them not to think about a quick return, but to settle down for the long haul. The prophet advised this approach in a remarkable letter to the exiles (Jer. 29). Here he urged them to face facts without being overwhelmed by them, as if to say, "You are where you are: bloom where you're planted". He encouraged them to make the most of living in exile, to build their homes, raise their families and seek work for their living in ways consistent with faith in Yahweh. If you seek the peace and prosperity of the city and if you can bring yourselves to pray for it, then you will prosper too, says the prophet.

He urged them to face facts without being overwhelmed by them.

Trust God for the future. "I know the plans I have for

you" declares the Lord, "... plans to give you hope and a future" (Jer. 29:11). Jeremiah offers hope beyond exile in the wonderful promise of a new covenant in which God would work to change His people from the inside-out, creating a truly faithful covenant community (Jer. 31:31).

In fact, this possibility of restoration and salvation even beyond the judgment of exile from the Land had been remarkably anticipated by Moses even before the people got into the land. Even more remarkably, the saving possibilities which Moses envisaged for the future made no mention of the sacrificial system as a means of expunging the sin of Israel's deep-rooted covenant unfaithfulness and disobedience. Instead Moses hints at an astonishing new kind of covenant arrangement. In this the command to "circumcise your hearts" (Deut. 10:16) becomes transformed into a promise of what God will do – "I will circumcise your hearts" (Deut. 30:6). It was this seed that came to flower in Jeremiah's vision.

It was Ezekiel, himself a deportee to Babylon, who added a further impetus to the hopes of the exiles. He describes to them a vision he has seen on the banks of the canal in Babylon in which the glory of God appears swirling in on his mobile chariot throne. God is not dead but alive, He is not absent but gloriously with us even here in exile, the prophet is able to tell the exiled community. Later Ezekiel prophesies of the radical work God will do to restore and save His people. He will act by His creative Spirit to replace the hard, rebellious hearts of His people into soft, responsive hearts, so making them into a new covenant people. He will put the Spirit of life into His "dead" people, in what amounts to an act of "resurrection"! (Ezek. 36–37).

165

Deuteronomy	< 800 years >	Jeremiah
old covenant affirmed on the time of entry to the Land		new covenant promised at the time of exile from the Land

The prophets of the Exile took seriously the fact that not only the people but the kings also had failed. With the demise of Israel's last king at the hands of the Babylonians hopes began to be raised that a new kind of kingship would emerge.

Both Jeremiah and Ezekiel looked forward to the day when God's new covenant people would be ruled by God's new Davidic king, the ideal Messianic ruler (Jer. 23; Ezek. 34). To Ezekiel it is unclear whether God will send a Davidic prince or come in person to do the job of bringing His kingdom in.

The prophet Isaiah gathers up all these various strands into a wonderful message of good news (Isa. 40:9). God will come in person to take up His rightful place as king once again (Isa. 40:3; 52:7). God will lead His people out of slavery to sin, eclipsing the deliverance from Egypt (Isa. 43–44). God will do all this through the obedient suffering and sacrificial death of a mysterious Servant-King (Isa. 42–53). Eventually, the salvation God has in mind will be tantamount to a renewal of all His created works (Isa. 65–66).

The prophetic sequence of salvation then looks like this: new exodus to new covenant to new kingship to new

creation. This is the theological sequence which the New Testament apostles worked to in unfolding the implications of the gospel of Jesus. Paul certainly is shadowing this scheme of salvation. For example, in 2 Corinthians chapters 1–6 and in Romans 8.

Let's look briefly at how this might work out. The return from Exile in Babylon to Jesus' entry into Jerusalem are the two events which frame the readings in *Cover to Cover*. These two events are five hundred years apart. So what on earth connects them? It's "Exile and Restoration".

As we saw in Isaiah, for Israel to return to the Land was one thing; to return to the Lord, quite another. God achieved the first through His unlikely agent, Cyrus, the pagan Medo-Persian conqueror of Babylonia whose edict sent the exiles home (see 2 Chron. 36; Ezra 1). But the second – the restoration of His people to covenant faithfulness – remained a larger need and hope even after the return to the Land began in 536 BC.

In the five hundred years between our two "bookend" events, a growing number of Jews began to believe that though they were indeed back in the Land, they were in effect still "in exile". This is acknowledged in post-Exilic Scriptures. "We are slaves … even in the land" (Ezra 9:9; Neh. 9:36). As Daniel prayed about the seventy years' limit on exile promised by Jeremiah, he is told of its extension to 490 years! (Dan. 9:24). Later Jewish Apocryphal writings preceding the New Testament echo this realisation (e.g. Baruch c.150 BC) and the Dead Sea Scrolls.

Two things prompted this recognition.
1: Except for a brief period under the Maccabees, Israel had remained subject to foreign domination – from Persian through Greek to Roman – which suggested

therefore that Israel remained under the judgment of God for her sins.

2: The glorious hopes of restoration and promises of salvation beyond exile, first projected in Deuteronomy 30:1–8 and amplified in the Exilic prophets (e.g. Jer. 31–33; Ezek. 34–37; Isa. 40–55), had evidently not yet materialised.

It was one of the claims of the "Covenanters" at Qumran who left us the "Dead Sea Scrolls", that they were at last the long-awaited new covenant community. In this sense the condition of "exile" remained a persistent awareness in Jewish thinking right up to the time of Jesus. In the words of the leading New Testament scholar, N.T. Wright: "Most Jews of this period … believed that, in all senses which mattered, Israel's exile was still in progress. Although she had come back from Babylon, the glorious message of the prophets remained unfulfilled. Israel still remained in thrall to foreigners; worse, Israel's God had not returned to Zion."

Jesus announces the end of exile in the forgiveness of sins.

The undiminished reality of exile and the unsatisfied longing for new covenant restoration thus forms the vivid backdrop for the coming of Jesus and the best window through which to grasp His significance.

Isaiah's long-awaited signal for the end of exile and start of restoration (the "voice crying in the wilderness" – Isaiah 40) is linked by all the Evangelists with the ministry and message of John the Baptist, as he seeks to prepare Israel for the coming of God's kingdom through God's agent, Jesus. So Jesus announces the end of exile in the forgiveness of sins and the welcome to outcasts to come home to God. He inaugurates the restoration of Israel by appointing the Twelve as His chosen heads of the renewed people of God. He obliquely refers to Himself as Isaiah's Suffering Servant, the mysterious agent of salvation.

In His final parables, such as the Tenants, He speaks not so much of His second coming but of His first coming as the arrival of the Lord and Master to call His people to account. Mark 12 makes this explicit. In the shadow of death, He will inaugurate the new covenant, promised by Jeremiah, through His own blood and go to the cross to bear the "curse" (Deut. 29:25–28) of exile and judgment in place of God's rebellious people.

It is with this ministry behind Him and this destiny ahead of Him, that we see Jesus climbing up to the Jerusalem and entering the city. After all, where else would Israel's King go to be crowned and then rebuild God's Temple? Where else would Israel's God return to in order to re-establish His saving rule? And the "death" and "resurrection" of God's people, envisaged by Ezekiel as the means by which ultimate salvation will come, is something Jesus enacts "solo", not as a mere figure of speech but as a stark reality.

The release of the Spirit at Pentecost as described in Acts 2 is, therefore, to be viewed not so much as the birth of the Church, as it is the renewal of Israel as the new covenant people of God. To this forgiven, cleansed, Spirit-filled people – according to the Exilic prophets' perspective – God would rapidly add the Gentiles who repent and believe.

BibleLives

Esther

The life of Esther is an extraordinary story where God's sovereignty merges with human responsibility and courage. Such a merge shows how God has committed, and to an extent, limited Himself to work with and through human beings. We see this principle first in Eden where Adam and Eve were given responsibility to "rule" over creation (Gen. 1:26–28) and "work in the garden and take care of it" (Gen. 2:15). They were to fill the earth and bring it under their influence and control.

An interesting commentary on man's responsibility is found in Proverbs 24:30–31 (TLB), "I walked by the field of a certain lazy fellow and saw that it was overgrown with thorns, and covered with weeds; and its walls were broken down." In other words, God does not (normally) step in to make up for man's laziness or cowardice. In this context, God has provided seed, soil, water and sunshine – everything necessary for a bountiful harvest. This is an example of His sovereign provision. The blessing of the harvest will only be realised however when man fulfils his own responsibility to prepare the ground, plant, tend, reap, winnow and bake.

Esther came from humble and obscure origins in the sense that she was an orphan and had to rely on the generosity and charity of her cousin Mordecai (Esth. 2:7). It is often said that power and wealth are very corrupting influences, yet Esther was untouched by their effects. Even though she now lived in a palace she never forgot her fellow Jews who lived under persecution. In fact both

Mordecai and Esther realised that God had raised her to a position of influence "for such a time as this" (Esth. 4:14). Here was God's sovereignty; now the question was, how would Esther respond – cowardice or courage?

We need to remember that even though she was the Queen, to enter the king's presence unbidden was against the law and punishable by death. Remember too, that King Xerxes was an angry man who had already deposed one queen because she had displeased him!

Esther's attitude is the perfect example of an intercessor. She was not only willing to identify with her people but also to suffer their fate even if that meant death. Esther, as a member of the royal family and government, and as a member of the Jewish race could "stand in the gap" between the two in order to represent them both and plead for mercy. This is a wonderful picture of Jesus; "God is on one side and all the people on the other side, and Christ Jesus, himself man, is between them to bring them together, by giving his life for all mankind" (1 Tim. 2:5 TLB).

One of the keys to Esther's life was preparation. In Esther chapter 2 we read that she was "brought up" by Mordecai involving preparation of her character, wisdom and education. We also discover there was a preparation of her physical appearance as she completed a 12-month beauty treatment and then was prepared by Hegai to be presented to King Xerxes. When Esther decided to enter the king's presence to plead for the Jews, she went through a period of spiritual preparation by fasting for three days along with her close friends. Finally, before actually presenting her request she prepared the king by creating two sumptuous feasts so that he would be more inclined to be responsive to her petition.

God himself had been preparing the king in various ways including giving him a sleepless night when he read of his deliverance from assassination by the Jew Mordecai. The Jews then prepared for attack by their enemies by gathering together and arming themselves.

Just as preparation was a key to Esther's life it is also a key to us today. We need to be prepared for battle by arming ourselves with the sword of the Spirit, which is the Word of God and prayer. Above all else, however, we have been chosen from humble origins by a king to be his bride for eternity and we have the wonderful privilege of preparing ourselves with a beauty of character and holiness for that glorious heavenly marriage (Rev. 19:7–8).

Esther

What I have noticed in Esther is that her name could mean favour. She seemed to be finding favour with the king throughout; when she became queen, when she went to ask the king to come to a special meal even though he hadn't called for her. And to think that what might have happened when the king found out she was a Jew! I would have thought something really terrible would happen but then again she found favour in the king's sight.

COVER TO COVER RESPONDS
In Esther the name of God appears as an acrostic five times! "Jehovah" appears in the ancient Hebrew text in chapter 1:20, 5:4, 5:13 and 7:7 and "Lord" appears in 7:5. Some commentators believe this is an example of the application of Deuteronomy 31:16–18, where God said He would hide His face if His people forsook Him. But though He was hidden from them He was still working for them, and if they really looked hard they would see both His hand of providence and His name. In the hidden plotting of Israel's enemies, God hid Himself to overrule. One wonderful application of this truth is that when you are going through difficult times and cannot see God, take courage, He has promised never to leave you or forsake you and He is there, hidden, working all things together for good.

FORUM VOICE
Praise Him for the great lessons He is teaching us! These comments encourage me to realise that even when things get tough I can rest, assured that God is still there and that He is making all things work for my good. What a great encouragement.

On Reflection

- What specific purpose do you feel God has called you for and how are you preparing for it?

- How can you apply the lesson from Esther into your own life situations?

- What is your own experience of God's love; just up to your ankles or deep waters to swim in?

- What oppositions to prayer do you face? Do you overcome them like Daniel or give in and tend not to pray?

- How do you balance time for yourself and family compared to time for the Lord and His work?

- How important are women in the purposes of God? What role do women play in your own church?

- How important is fasting? What role does it play in your own life and church?

- How do you respond when people ridicule your beliefs and your efforts to share your faith?

- What is your favourite section of Psalm 119 and why?

- Do you believe in tithing? What are your reasons?

CommentOn   *Cover to Cover* Forum

http://www.cover2cover.org/docs/forhome.htm

10

The Gospel of a New Age

The Eagle's Word

From the early days of the Church John's Gospel acquired the symbol of "the eagle". The great scholar Jerome (349–420 AD) identified each of the four Gospels with one of the four creatures seen by Ezekiel in vision (Ezek. 1 and 10). He chose the eagle for John.

As an eagle sweeps through the skies in majestic flight, so John's Gospel, again and again, soars up to heaven and swoops back to earth, telling the story of Jesus the Christ. Jesus uniquely, as John presents Him, embodies Israel's human vocation and incarnates Israel's God, the One Creator God of the world.

The author?

Broadly speaking there are three approaches to the question: who wrote John's Gospel? All three interact with the identity of the character described as the "Beloved Disciple" (13:23 – where he is in the Upper Room, which would suggest that he is one of the Twelve; 19:26; 20:2; 21:7; 21:24):

> **Jesus uniquely embodies Israel's human vocation and incarnates Israel's God, the One Creator God of the world.**

(i) The first view denies that John, the Apostle, the Son of Zebedee, is to be identified with the "Beloved Disciple". It is strange that so much of the Galilean ministry of Jesus is omitted by the author (though one answer recently offered is that John wrote consciously knowing that his readers had Mark's Gospel already in their hands – Richard Bauckham). This view suggests that the Beloved Disciple, himself a Jewish disciple of Jesus, wrote the Gospel, building on his own eye-witness recollections.

Insight

(ii) The second view is that a follower of the Apostle John, a member of a supposed "Johannine Circle or School or Community" used the reminiscences of the Apostle. This leaves open the identity of the "Beloved Disciple" whom some have suggested may even have been Lazarus (11:3,11,36 with 21:23).

(iii) The traditional view – defended in recent times by Don Carson among others – is that John the Evangelist is the Apostle John, the Son of Zebedee, who is himself the "Beloved Disciple". It is worth noting that Johannine scholarship spent the first half of the twentieth century fixated on the idea that John was a very Greek, very late and therefore very unhistorical Gospel, now largely considers it to be Jewish, much earlier, perhaps even an independent source to the Synoptics, and therefore based on reliable historical knowledge (21:24).

Even a cursory reading of the four Gospels makes you realise how different John's Gospel is. John has no parables, no Sermon on the Mount, no Transfiguration, no Last Supper or Gethsemane.

Gary Burge sums up the debate by saying: "The hypothesis that John, the Son of Zebedee is the beloved disciple – and the Gospel's eyewitness – fits well. [But], even though the apostle John was no doubt the fountain-head of the Gospel's traditions, its text was subsequently edited and re-forged by disciples within the Johannine church."

So when was it written? Carson, Morris and Moo – in the standard evangelical introduction to the New Testament writings, tentatively suggest a date in the region of 80–85 AD. This allows room for the Epistles of John to be dated somewhat later and to view them as perhaps correcting "gnostic" misunderstandings and misuse of John's Gospel (Burge).

The uniqueness of John's Gospel

Even a cursory reading of the four Gospels makes you realise how different John's Gospel is. John has no parables, no Sermon on the Mount, no Transfiguration, no Last Supper or Gethsemane. Instead, he has Jesus delivering lengthy discourses and, unlike the Synoptics, going out of His way to draw attention to Himself.

However, these differences can be overdrawn; there is nothing in John that cannot be shown to exist in some form in the other three Gospels. Like them, John is speaking about the same historical Jesus and – apart from his placement of the Temple incident – following essentially the same outline of the story. In fact it is to John's mention of three Passover feasts that we owe our view of Jesus' ministry as lasting three years and not one year.

How to Characterise John's Gospel
The Gospel of Word and Wisdom

The overture in John 1:1–18, contains all the seeds of subsequent development in the Gospel. John clothes his "logos" in the categories used to describe God's "wisdom" both in the Old Testament and in Jewish writings contemporary to Jesus (Proverbs 8; Ecclesiasticus 24). The "wisdom" terminology was very influential for John and other New Testament writers. It enabled the unprecedented step of joining the life and activity of a human being (Jesus of Nazareth) with the life and activity of the One Creator God within the acceptable framework of Jewish monotheism (Col. 1:15–20; Heb. 1:1–4).

John might well have said: "In the beginning was

wisdom" (*sophia*) but for his own good reasons he chose "word" (*logos*). By doing so he lost none of the useful resonance the term had in Greek philosophy but maintained the crucial connection with the Old Testament. There God's "word" effects creation (Gen. 1:1; Ps. 33:6) and brings revelation through the prophets. "Word" has the added significance of referring also to the preaching of the gospel message, the "word" of Christ (Acts 4:4, 29; 8:25; 12:24; Rom. 10:8–17; 1 Thess. 1:5–6; Col. 1:5).

The Gospel of Glory
John wants to portray the whole of Jesus' life and ministry as demonstrating the glory of God (1:14). This is perhaps, why, surprisingly, he omits to mention the Transfiguration account as told in the Synoptics. For John, Jesus is not so much transfigured on one occasion but translucent all the way through His ministry. Strikingly, John highlights the Cross as the highpoint of His exaltation (3:14; 8:28; 12:32).

> **Jesus fulfils and replaces the significance and purpose of all of Israel's feasts and institutions.**

The Gospel of Fulfilment
Jesus fulfils and replaces the significance and purpose of all of Israel's feasts and institutions and so brings the whole Scriptural narrative of the Old Testament to its intended goal and climax. It is in this comprehensive and conclusive way that the "Scriptures testify" to Jesus (5:39). This involves a radical break with Judaism and the inauguration of a whole new order of things – making John the Gospel of the New Age.

Overture
Creation/New creation (1:1–18)
New Covenant (1:16–51)

New Wine for a New Age (2:1–11)
New Temple (2:12ff.)
New Birth (3:1ff.)
New Water.
New Worship (4)
New Sabbath (5)
New Exodus and Bread from Heaven (6)
New Tabernacles; new Light and Water (7–8)
New Shepherd (9–10)
New Creation (11) – Resurrection!

Transition Section
New Way to Glory (11:50–12:50)
New Commandment (13)
New life in the Spirit for the New Covenant community
(14–16)
New High Priest (17)
New Enthronement as King on the Cross (18–19)
New Creation initiated in Resurrection (20–21)

The Gospel of Crisis
John presents the death of Jesus as bringing the world to
a point of crisis; judgment for it and for its "ruler" (12:31).
Jesus has been portrayed as "on trial", drawing on the law
court imagery of Isaiah 40–55.

In Isaiah, Yahweh is both the judge and a party in the
dispute. He calls on the pagan gods to prove themselves
and His people, Israel, to "bear witness" to Him (Isa.
41:1–5, 21–29; 43:8–13; 44:6–8; 45:20–25). In John's
account, Jesus is a party to the dispute but also is seen
to be the judge, thus standing in the place of Yahweh.
Tragically and ironically it is God's own people, Israel,
who now testify against Him! (see especially 5:16–47).
Jesus is the true "witness" who is the final revelation of
the one true God (3:11). To have seen Him is to see the
Father (14:9–10).

The Gospel of the Resurrection

"After he was raised from the dead, his disciples recalled what he had said. Then they believed the Scripture and the words that Jesus had spoken" (2:21–22). John is "writing his Gospel from a vantage-point he did not himself enjoy during Jesus' earthly ministry" (William Lane). Only in the light of the resurrection could Jesus be properly understood.

The Gospel of the Holy Spirit

It is with the hindsight of the Holy Spirit that Jesus is seen in His full glory (John 7:37–39). It is the Spirit who glorifies Jesus and leads the disciples into the deeper and developing truth about Jesus (John 16:12–15). John's own Gospel is an example of this very promise. For this reason John's Gospel proved to be – and continues to be – "an empowering Gospel that shaped this Christian community so that it would expect dynamic spiritual experiences. Jesus and the Father were dwelling within these spiritually reborn believers (14:23). No other Gospel speaks like this" (Gary Burge).

> **The way to enjoy this life is to believe, and go on believing, that Jesus is the Christ.**

The Gospel of Life and Faith

John speaks sparingly of the kingdom of God, choosing to emphasise the present experience of the kingdom of God. In terms of having and enjoying eternal life now (3:16, 36; 5:21). The way to enjoy this life is to believe (1:12–13), and go on believing, that Jesus is the Christ.

Faith for John is both a believing that Jesus is the Christ – and a believing in making a radical commitment to Jesus and enjoying an intimate relationship with Him. "Now

Jesus did many other signs in the presence of his disciples which are not written in this book. But these are
written so that you may believe that Jesus is the Messiah,
the Son of God, and that through believing you may have
life in his name" (20:30–31).

For Further Reading
Don Carson, *The Gospel According to John* (IVP 1991) –
among all the many commentaries on John's Gospel this
is the single most valuable volume for the general,
thoughtful reader. Theologically rich and exegetically
astute, this is a vibrant and faith-nourishing study, as are
most things Carson writes.

Ben Witherington, *John's Wisdom* (Lutterworth 1995) –
this too is accessible to the general reader, and interprets
the Gospel consistently through the lens of OT/Jewish
Wisdom theology.

John Pryor, *John the Evangelist of the Covenant People*
(Darton, Longman and Todd, 1992) – this is the work that
has helped me most and is quite outstanding, especially
in drawing out the fulfilment of the Old Testament in
John's presentation of Jesus.

Kevin Quast, *Reading the Gospel of John* (Paulist Press,
1991) – one of a series of clear and simple guides to the
biblical books, written with disarming and unobtrusive
but excellent scholarship, with helpful graphs and charts.

Gary Burge, *The Anointed Community – the Holy Spirit
in John* (Eerdmans, 1987) – exhaustive and inspiring.

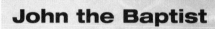

John the Baptist

John is one of the few characters whose life was the subject of prophecy hundreds of years before he was born. In Luke 3:3–6 we read that his ministry fulfilled the announcement in Isaiah 40:3–5 of one who would come to prepare the way of the Lord. Even before he was conceived, an angel explained that the child had to be given a special name. It would have been normal for him to be called after his father, Zechariah, meaning "Remembered of the Lord". However, the child was to have a totally different name, John, meaning "God is gracious".

This choice of name was such a marked departure from custom that the neighbours argued against it and were astonished when dumb Zechariah wrote his name on a tablet (Luke 1:61–63). These names are highly significant and mark a departure from family tradition and from the Old Testament law of sacrifice to the New Testament salvation by grace. God was no longer to simply "remember" humankind but be "gracious" to them.

For nearly 1,500 years since the writing of Leviticus the only way to approach God was by presenting a special blood sacrifice and keeping the Laws of Moses. Now a son of the priesthood, John, ushered in a new way of approaching God who graciously provided His own Son as that blood sacrifice. John himself declared, "For Moses gave us only the Law with its rigid demands and merciless justice, while Jesus Christ brought us loving [merciful] forgiveness as well" (John 1:17 TLB).

John's message of repentance was complemented by the promise of the coming of the Messiah and the baptism of the Holy Spirit.

John's character and ministry is full of apparent contradiction. His preaching is bold and fiery, as in Luke 3:7: "You brood of snakes! You are trying to escape hell without truly turning to God!" (TLB); yet he also says in Mark 1:7, "Someone is coming soon who is far greater than I am, so much greater that I am not even worthy to be his slave" (TLB). Here is an indication of true humility, which is not so much an attitude of subservience to others but more an attitude of willing obedience and servanthood to an all-powerful God.

John declared of Jesus, "He must become greater and greater, and I must become less and less" (John 3:30 TLB). He was not preoccupied with his own ministry but clearly directed his disciples to follow Jesus instead.

It was John's forthright preaching that led to his eventual martyrdom when he criticised Herod for his relationship with his brother's wife (Matt. 14:1–12). In his humble obedience to God, John refused to be silenced by the fear of man but boldly spoke out against sin even in the lives of powerful leaders.

John's life is an inspiration to us today. He was a faithful preacher of God's gracious way of salvation, always pointing away from himself to Jesus. His life and witness prepared people's hearts to recognise and repent of their sin so they could receive Jesus as their Saviour. We may not be called to wear strange clothes in a desert but we are all called to boldly proclaim the message of grace so others can receive God's salvation by faith in Jesus.

Mary and Martha

Mary and Martha go together like oil and water, or chalk and cheese. Although they are sisters, and usually appear together in the Bible, its authors often draw attention to their differences rather than their similarities. Martha seems to be more of a practical, extrovert temperament and Mary has a devotional, introvert personality. Whilst both of these dispositions are perfectly normal, there seem to be underlying insecurities and incorrect priorities in Martha's heart that are not found in Mary. In fact, at one point, Jesus remarked that Mary had chosen a better course of action than Martha, which was due to correct priorities, not different temperaments.

A similar example of contrasting the attitude of siblings occurs with Jacob and Esau in the Old Testament. In Genesis 25:29–34 Esau traded his birthright inheritance as the older brother for a bowl of stew. That birthright included the spiritual and tribal leadership that had been passed down from Abraham and yet, in the words of The Living Bible, Esau "went on about his business, indifferent to the loss of the rights he had thrown away" (Gen. 25:34). Esau's focus was on the physical, material world which he made a priority over the spiritual but invisible inheritance that truly belonged to him. He chose the immediate pleasure of food to eternal fellowship with God.

Consider now the story of Mary and Martha in Luke 10:38–42. Many people sympathise with Martha and feel

Mary was lazy whilst her sister was faithfully preparing food for Jesus and the other guests. Certainly Martha felt this way and even asked Jesus to rebuke her sister! We need to read the text carefully to really understand why this story has been included in the Scriptures. This is not just a minor family dispute but a drama of fundamental significance to our faith and relationship with God. The Amplified version translates Luke 10:40 thus, "Martha, over occupied and too busy, was distracted with much serving." Jesus responds to her in verse 41, "Martha, Martha, you are anxious and troubled about many things".

These statements give us a window of insight into Martha's attitudes and priorities. Rather than prepare something quickly and simply for Jesus, it is suggested that Martha was so preoccupied about preparing an elaborate meal to impress and earn His commendation, that she had no time to spend with Jesus Himself. Work for the Lord distracted Martha and became more important to her than spending time with the Lord of the Work! Like Esau, she chose food instead of fellowship.

This is a similar thought to the story of the church at Ephesus found in Revelation 2:1–6. "I see what you've done, your hard, hard work, your refusal to quit. I know you can't stomach evil … I know your persistence, your courage in my cause, that you never wear out". Yet Jesus charged them, "you have left and abandoned the love that you had at first – you have deserted me your first love" (*The Message*). Ephesus was a place where the believers worked so hard for the church of the Lord that they had abandoned the Lord of the Church! It is not unlike a marriage where the partners cook, clean, garden and decorate but there is no longer any romance. If we are not careful we can, like the Pharisees, be so concerned about the beautiful temple that we ignore the One for whom it was built.

The correct priority for our lives is shown in Mark 3:14: "He appointed twelve ... that they might be with him and that he might send them out to preach". We spend time in fellowship with Jesus and then go to work. Mary did not avoid work, she simply chose to be at the feet of Jesus. If those feet were still, she too would be still but if those feet were moving with a sense of purpose she would walk with Jesus to work with Him. Mary listened to Jesus' words of encouragement and then obeyed His words of direction. The story of Mary and Martha helps reveal to us the twin characteristics in our lives: to worship the Lord and work for Him. The example of Mary is that fellowship should always come first.

Missing Link

Have you ever wondered what happened between
Malachi and Matthew? In our journey through *Cover to
Cover* we have followed a fairly continuous storyline, but
suddenly there is a gap of around 400 years! In Malachi
the Jews, under Persian rule, worship in the Jerusalem
Temple led by the High Priest descended from Aaron. In
Matthew, the Jews worship primarily in synagogues and
the priesthood is led by a rich aristocracy. The Jewish
Scriptures have been translated into Greek and the Land
is now part of the Roman Empire. The purpose of this
special feature is to provide the missing link between
these two books and show how and when all these
changes happened.

InDetail

538—444 BC
The area of Israel and much of the Middle East is ruled
by Persia. Small groups of Jews led by Zerrubabel, Ezra
and Nehemiah return from captivity to rebuild the Temple
and walls of Jerusalem. The priesthood is based on
ancestry from Aaron. As Jews returned to the Land
weekly meetings were organised in towns and villages
where the Torah or Law was read and explained. These
were the forerunners of synagogues which eventually
became the religious centre in every village.

---

333 BC
Greece became the dominant power as Alexander the
Great conquers Persia and rules the known world. He
begins a process of Hellenisation so Greek thought,
culture and language are extended throughout his empire.
After Alexander's death the eastern territories were

divided between the Seleucids who ruled in Syria and the Ptolemies who ruled in Egypt. It was the latter who became responsible for the land of Israel.

290 BC
The Jewish Scriptures were translated into Greek, a version known as the Septuagint which was later read in the time of Jesus and quoted in the New Testament.

198 BC
Antiochus III of Syria defeats Egypt and gains control of Israel.

175 BC
Antiochus Epiphanes of Syria bans Judaism, kills many Jews and sacrifices a pig on the altar of the Temple in Jerusalem. (Some Bible scholars see this as a fulfilment of Daniel 11:31.)

167 BC
Mattathias leads a Jewish revolt against Syria. He and his sons, particularly Judas "the Maccabee" ("hammer") were successful and on 25th Kislev 164 BC they re-dedicated the Temple in Jerusalem. This event has been commemorated ever since by the Festival of Hanukkah or Lights (see John 10:22). Under the Maccabees who founded the Hasomonean dynasty the rulers also took over the position of High Priest. During this whole period the

position of the priesthood was the subject of great rivalry and based on political expediency rather than Aaronic descent.

130 BC

Emergence of the Pharisees who were ultra orthodox Jews and the liberal Sadducees who were Hellenized Jews of the aristocracy. It was about this time that the Sanhedrin was established as the ruling authority of the Jewish religion.

130—104 BC

John Hyracanus, the next Hasomonean ruler of Israel, extends the territory of the Jewish state to include Idumea which is OT Edom.

65 BC

Antipater, an Edomite, is governor of Idumea.

63 BC

The Roman general Pompey invades Palestine and captures Jerusalem. The Jews again lose their independence and are ruled by a foreign power.

37 BC

Herod the Great, son of Antipater, part Edomite and part

Jew is appointed by Rome as king of Judea.

20 BC
Herod begins rebuilding the Temple in Jerusalem.

0
Herod the Great dies and his kingdom is bequeathed to three of his sons – Judea and Samaria to Archelaus (Matt. 2:22), Galilee and Perea to Herod-Antipas, and his NE territories to Philip (Luke 3:1). The land is under Roman occupation whilst the priesthood is controlled by the Jewish aristocracy and is largely concerned with politics and commerce. The revival of Jehovah worshipping Pharisees becomes bogged down in religious ritual and pride. The Sanhedrin is dominated by the Sadducees who deny the supernatural, e.g. angels and resurrection of the dead (Acts 23:6–8).

Commitment Over All Others

FORUM VOICE

In Luke 14:26, what did Jesus mean when he said "If anyone comes to me and does not hate his father and mother, his wife and children, his brothers and sisters – yes, even his own life – he cannot be my disciple"? I'm obviously missing the intent of this verse. I know that Jesus would not want us to literally hate anyone, but I just can't grasp what this is supposed to tell me.

COVER TO COVER RESPONDS

One of the ways I like to study the Bible is by reading the same verses in different translations. In The Living Bible Luke 14:26 reads, "Anyone who wants to be my follower must love me far more than he does his own father ..."; in *The Message*, "Anyone who comes to me but refuses to let go of father ..."; in the Amplified, "If anyone comes to me and does not hate his own father and mother, that is in the sense of indifference to or relative disregard for them in comparison with his attitude toward God". Also look at the context of the verse in relation to the passage where it occurs, which in this case is dealing with total commitment to Christ in Luke 14:16–34.

The sense of the passage is repeated with a slight variation in Matthew 10:37: "He who loves and takes more pleasure in father or mother than me" (Amplified). From these readings I believe the message is clear – we are to love Jesus more than any other person, ambition or even our own life. We are to love others, especially our parents, (Mark 12:31; Eph. 6:1) but wherever there is a conflict and a choice we are to love and follow Jesus and refuse to love and follow the other influence. For example, some Christians have obeyed the call of God and chosen to be missionaries instead of entering the family business, whilst others have refused to love their own lives more than Christ and have been martyred for their faith. If you think about it this is only an extension of the first commandment, "You shall have no other gods before me". A word of caution – this principle must never be used as a false excuse to avoid family responsibilities (Matt. 15:3–8 and 1 Tim. 5:8).

193

God's Humour

FORUM VOICE

We know biblically that God loves, cares, guides, disciplines etc. I would like to know whether He can also show humour to His children.

COVER TO COVER RESPONDS

Humour, like beauty, can often be in the eye of the beholder. There are also different types of humour such as farce, sarcasm, slapstick, satire, clown, wit, irony etc. In Psalm 2:4 it does say that God laughs, and some would see a sense of humour in God choosing weak and insignificant people to proclaim His kingdom and confound the strong and proud (1 Cor. 1:26–28). Hebrew slaves such as Joseph and Daniel could interpret dreams that the professional magicians could not.

Another example could be Haman who had to praise his enemy Mordecai and was hanged on the very gallows he had built to hang Mordecai on (Esth. 6:1–7:10). In a number of passages God presents truth in a humorous way. For example, Peter, a fisherman, was sent to catch a fish that would have a coin in its mouth which would pay the tax! I do not believe that God plays jokes on us but I think He does have a sense of humour and although His presence may not be a place of continual funny stories it is a place of continual joy (Neh. 8:10; Ps. 16:11).

FORUM VOICE

I think that the way that Jesus answered the Pharisees was quite humorous and showed quick-wittedness.

The Jesus Genealogies

FORUM VOICE
   In Matthew 9:9, Matthew was mentioned as the tax collector. In Mark 2:14 and in Luke 5:27 is Levi referring to the same Matthew? If so, what is the relationship between James and Matthew, as in Mark 3:18 James was referred to as the son of Alphaeus? Also under Day 274 of the *Cover to Cover* guide, one of the references refers to two genealogies of Jesus, is Luke 3:23–38 referring to Mary's lineage?

COVER TO COVER RESPONDS
   Well spotted. It seems that James and Matthew could have been brothers because the name of their father is the same, Alphaeus; although of course there could have been two fathers of the same name, just as there were a number of women called Mary. Commentators do consider it a possibility that they were brothers although it is not specifically stated in Scripture.

The genealogies of Jesus are fascinating, not least because of their differences. The Matthew list is the regal legal line tracing Jesus as a Jew from Abraham, Judah (Gen. 49:10) and on through David from whom it was prophesied the king of an everlasting kingdom would come (1 Sam. 7). The natural line is through Heli the father of Mary and whose son-in-law Joseph became. This fulfilled the prophecy in Genesis 3:15 that the Messiah would be the "seed of a woman" and links Jesus not only as a Jew but also as the offspring of Adam and therefore representative of the entire human race.

Also the Luke list traces Jesus through Nathan, the son of David and Bathsheba and not through Solomon (1 Chron. 3:5). This is because God had sworn that none of Jehoiakim's descendants would ever rule in Israel (Jer. 22:24–30). Jehoiakim was a descendant of Solomon and God went back to a different son of David to establish the Messianic line rather than through the rebellious kings that came through Solomon.

There are in fact three genealogies of Jesus in the NT. We must never forget John 1:1, "In the beginning was the

Word, and the Word was with God, and the Word was God", and John 1:14, "The Word became flesh and dwelt among us, and we beheld His glory, the glory as of the only begotten of the Father, full of grace and truth" (NKJ).

Holy Communion

FORUM VOICE
I have been pondering on John 6:54–56 for the last few days and the more I looked at it, the more I feel that there is a deeper significance than what has been commonly interpreted to be the forgiveness of sins and the taking of the flesh and blood in "Holy Communion", or the dying to self and resurrection. I wonder if you could shed some light on the above passage.

COVER TO COVER RESPONDS
In my view this passage is not just referring to the sacrificial death of Jesus but also the establishment of a new covenant, whereby God promises to write His laws in a new heart that He will give us (Jer. 31:31–34; Ezek. 36:26). Jesus' blood cleanses us from sin (Eph. 1:7) but also establishes an everlasting covenant (Luke 22:19–20; Heb. 13:20). There are different types of covenant, but at its most powerful covenant relates to one life lived out through two bodies. For example, in marriage, the partners of the marriage covenant are to become "one flesh" which is not just a reference to sexual union but a union of heart, will and purpose.

When we take bread and wine therefore we are not just remembering the sacrifice of Jesus for our sins but that "we have been crucified with Christ and that we no longer live, but Christ lives in me" (Gal. 2:20). In this sense, a Christian is not just someone who admires the teachings of Jesus, is inspired by His selfless life or is thrilled with His miracles, but someone in whom Christ lives and who lives in Christ as a branch in the vine (John 15). This is a huge and fascinating subject, I hope these brief thoughts help.

The Time Has Come

In John chapter 2 at the wedding in Cana when Jesus said His hour had not yet come, what did He mean? I thought He was trying to say that it wasn't yet time for Him to show Himself, but He still went ahead to turn water into wine. Does this mean that His statement meant something else?

COVER TO COVER RESPONDS

The Gospel of John often refers to the concept of a special time in the life of Jesus. In some references His time has not yet come (John 2:4; 7:6; 8:30; 8:20) and other verses show that His time has come (John 12:23; 13:1; 17:1). The "time" in question often seems to have been His sacrificial death on the cross, which secured our salvation, and it was always the ultimate focus of Jesus' life, even above His unparalleled teaching and unsurpassed miracles. Whatever else Jesus did paled into insignificance compared to His awareness of the time of His death that was yet to come.

In some cases Jesus seems to have said that He did not intend to act because His time had not yet come, but then He did indeed act soon afterwards. For example, in John 2 He did act and turned the water into wine, and in John 7:6–10 He did go to the feast even though He told the disciples He would not. In both cases Jesus may have been waiting to receive His Father's instructions, or referring to a delay because it was not yet quite the right time to act, rather than an absolute denial. The story in John 11 of the raising of Lazarus is an example of this when Jesus did not act for two days until He knew Lazarus was dead and God's purposes were served more effectively by a miracle of resurrection than a miracle of healing.

It is important that we learn to be sensitive to God's timing in our lives (Eccles. 3:1–8) or we might produce an Ishmael from our "Flesh" rather than an Isaac from our "Spirit" (Gal. 4:21–31) because we need not only faith but also patience to inherit God's promises for our lives (Heb. 6:12).

On Reflection

- What is your own definition of a good friend and how do you measure up to it?

- Do you tend to be a workaholic or do you regularly take time just to relax with people and be quiet before the Lord?

- How could you play an important part in showing hospitality to newcomers to your church?

- Is your life a good balance of work and worship?

- What can you do to "Prepare the way for the Lord" like John the Baptist?

- In what way do you see the miraculous and the practical combined in your own life and church?

- What obstacles do you need to push through to touch Jesus?

- Are there any people you have not forgiven?

- Do you have any doubts that you need to bring to Jesus?

- To what extent is materialism a problem in your life and culture?

CommentOn *Cover to Cover* Forum

http://www.cover2cover.org/docs/forhome.htm

199

11

Judas

BibleLives

The key lesson we draw from the life of Judas is not a picture of how to do things, but of how not to do things. In other words, his life is not one to be followed, but one to be avoided. The Bible purposefully contains many such negative examples including Cain murdering his brother and the Israelites dying in the wilderness because of their unbelief. The New Testament specifically recounts both these events as incidents that are useful for our spiritual instruction. If we can understand the factors that led to such actions we can more easily recognise them intruding into our own lives and therefore take steps at an early stage to prevent similar consequences.

There are a number of ways in which we could study the life of Judas but here we will concentrate on his attitude to money and how that impacted his whole personality. It is important at this stage to appreciate that no disciple was perfect and Judas was only one of twelve imperfect people. Thomas had his doubts, Simon Peter denied Christ and James and John sought positions as the greatest of the disciples.

Judas was one of the twelve sent out by Jesus with power and authority "to cure diseases, preach the kingdom and heal the sick" (Luke 9:1–2). He not only enjoyed the companionship of Jesus, heard His teaching first hand and saw Him work miracles, but Judas also healed the sick and experienced God's power at work through himself. Yet there was an area of Judas's life where he refused to change and allow God to work in his own heart.

In John 12:6 the New Testament reveals that Judas acted as treasurer for the travelling team of Jesus and the disciples. He kept their common funds and was responsible for paying for food or any other needs of the group. However, it also says that he had a problem with greed and so he "often dipped into [the funds] for his own use!" (TLB). The context of this verse is in the passage where Mary had anointed Jesus with expensive perfume and Judas objected at this waste suggesting that it could have been sold and the money given to the poor. His motive is revealed as greed because the perfume was worth a year's wages.

Greed not only seeks more for itself but is outraged when others have more. Judas is also revealed to have a hard heart because he did not care about the poor. Jesus' entire ministry was directed to preaching the good news to the poor and yet Judas had no compassion for them at all. If we are to be true followers of Jesus we have to follow His attitudes as well as His actions.

Many commentators have given different reasons why Judas betrayed Jesus. Some even feel that Judas wanted Jesus to use His miraculous powers to defeat the Romans and return Israel to Jewish control. The betrayal, arrest and imprisonment would therefore have forced Jesus to respond and fight against the authorities.

However, we know that Judas was a thief, greedy for money and 30 pieces of silver was a considerable temptation. Ephesians 4:27 advises us: "do not give the devil a foothold". Judas's previous activities of theft and hypocrisy had given satan a foothold in his life so with his spiritual defences down it was all too easy for the devil to "enter in" and persuade him to betray Jesus. It was only after the event that Judas realised the full horror of his actions and committed suicide.

Perhaps the first key lesson we can learn from his life are that "small" sins can give the devil a foothold and lead to other sins with much more serious consequences. Secondly, we should assess the possible consequences of our actions beforehand rather than after the event when it is too late. Finally, remember that Judas refused to repent and find forgiveness unlike the other disciples such as Thomas and Peter.

If there is an issue in your life, confess it and prevent it destroying both you and your faith. Scripture details Judas's life that we might not repeat his mistake but be loyal and holy disciples worthy of our Master.

Thomas

Thomas is well known as the disciple who doubted.
It has been suggested that people fall into a number of
categories in respect of their likelihood to believe. There
are those who believe anything, those who believe
nothing and those who, given sufficient evidence, are
prepared to move from unbelief to faith. This does not
just apply in the realm of religion but in other areas such
as newspaper and TV reports, product advertising claims
and so on.

There are those of us with a positive attitude who always
believe the best, and those who are pessimistic – always
assuming the worst. Most of us vacillate between these
two extremes but we will generally tend to one or the
other. In fact, it has been said that the more highly
educated and analytical we become, it is increasingly
likely that we will be inclined towards negativity and
scepticism. It is clear from the biblical record that Thomas
was of a negative disposition.

There are three particular incidents when Thomas
revealed his negative attitude to life. In John 10:22–39 the
Jewish leaders in Jerusalem tried to arrest and kill Jesus
who withdrew to a place of safety beyond the Jordan
river. It was after this in John 11:1–3 that a message was
sent to Jesus about the illness of Lazarus who lived just
outside Jerusalem in the village of Bethany. When Jesus
told the disciples in John 11:15 that He intended to return
to the Jerusalem area to visit the dead Lazarus it
prompted an immediate negative response from Thomas.

No doubt remembering the attempt to kill Jesus and suppress His teachings the last time He was in the area, Thomas said, "Let's go too – and die with him" (John 11:16 TLB).

Although his devotion and loyalty is commendable, Thomas clearly felt a deep pessimism about another journey into the stronghold of the hostile Jewish leaders. His doubts were actually well-founded, for it was the raising of Lazarus from the dead which galvanised the Pharisees into action and to plot the death of Jesus (John 11:45–53).

Later, in John 14:1–4, Jesus seeks to encourage His disciples and tells them, "You know where I am going and how to get there", but Thomas responds, "No we don't. We haven't any idea where you are going, so how can we know the way?" (TLB). It was his negative but honest response that then produced one of the most significant statements of Jesus when He graciously replied, "I am the way and the truth and the life".

Finally, Thomas refused to believe in the resurrection of Jesus: "Unless I see the nail holes in his hands, put my finger in the nail holes, and stick my hand in his side, I won't believe it" (John 20:25 *The Message*). Notice that for Thomas seeing was certainly not believing because just to see Jesus was insufficient – he had to actually touch His wounds before he could believe. It is surely encouraging for us today that such a confirmed sceptic as Thomas came to believe in the miracle of the resurrection – it really must have happened!

Thomas's actions have earned him the sobriquet "Doubting Thomas". This is both inaccurate and unfair. Even though he was a person of a negative and critical

disposition, he was sufficiently open-minded to change his views when presented with God's truth. Jesus graciously acceded to his request and Thomas became a fearless and outspoken witness of the power of the resurrection. That power could not only raise Jesus from the dead but it could also transform an unbelieving sceptic into a powerful preacher of the truth he had once denied.

If we are honest to God with our doubts then, like Thomas, He will make Himself real to us and help our unbelief. We are not called to be optimists, pessimists or even realists but simply people of faith the size of a mustard seed that can move mountains of doubt and unbelief.

God's Names

Have you noticed that as we read through the Bible God is addressed by different names? God has revealed Himself to us in many ways – through creation, through His Word, through His Holy Spirit, through His deeds, through His Son and through His Names. If we lack understanding in any one of these areas our perception of God may be incomplete and our spiritual life weakened. In the original Hebrew, God is revealed by many different names which lose their unique meanings when translated into English. These original meanings reveal inspiring aspects of God's character which can strengthen our faith and inflame our hearts! In the New International Version the translators have used a combination of words and capital letters to differentiate between the original Hebrew names as shown below:

ENGLISH		ORIGINAL HEBREW
God	Gen. 1:1	El, Elah or Elohim
LORD God	Gen. 2:7	Jehovah Elohim
God Most High	Gen. 14:19	El Elyon
Sovereign LORD	Gen. 15:2	Adonai Jehovah
God Almighty	Gen. 17:1	El Shaddai
Eternal God	Gen. 21:33	El Olam
LORD	Deut. 6:4	Jehovah
Lord	Neh. 1:11	Adonai
LORD Almighty (of hosts)	Jer. 29:21	Jehovah Sabaoth

The "EL" names of God

EL El means strength, so He is the STRONG ONE, or MIGHTY ONE as in Psalm 18:32, Job 36:5. The EL names are often used in terms of God as Creator and using His creative powers.

ELAH The STRONG ONE who is to be WORSHIPPED as in Ezra 7:19, Daniel 2:19,23.

ELOHIM From EL and ALAH. ALAH means to swear, to bind oneself by covenant and therefore implies faithfulness. ELOHIM means THE STRONG FAITHFUL ONE (who is to be TRUSTED, OBEYED and WORSHIPPED). ELOHIM is a uni-plural noun similar to "flock" which relates to one group of several sheep and is therefore an early biblical indication of the Trinity. In Genesis 1:26 it is ELOHIM who says "let US make man in OUR image".

EL ELYON HIGHEST or MOST HIGH. In Genesis 14:19 EL ELYON is the "Possessor of Heaven and Earth".

EL OLAM OLAM relates to time – "long ago" in Joshua 24:2 and to something hidden in 2 Kings 4:27 so EL OLAM is the God of SECRET THINGS in Deuteronomy 29:29 and of the MYSTERY OF TIME or the AGES as in Psalm 90:2,4. He is everlasting and no one can fully understand Him in Isaiah 40:28.

EL SHADDAI The STRONG SUFFICIENT ONE. It is suggested that SHADDAI relates to the breast and as a woman nourishing her child, and EL SHADDAI is the "Strong Pourer Forth" of life and blessing who produces growth and fruitfulness (Isa. 49:15). Thus it was to impotent Abram and Sarah that God said, "I am EL SHADDAI … I will multiply you exceedingly" (Gen. 17:1,2 NKJ). EL SHADDAI was "SUFFICIENT" to meet Abram's greatest need. In EL SHADDAI God's almightiness is of the breast not the sword; we see His loving provision not His awesome power.

EL ROI The STRONG ONE WHO SEES (and watches over me and intervenes on my behalf) – Genesis 16:13.

The "JEHOVAH" names of God

JEHOVAH The SELF-EXISTENT ONE WHO REVEALS HIMSELF.
Literally Jehovah means "I AM" and is usually found in conjunction
with other Hebrew words to reveal different aspects of God's
character. The Jehovah names are often used of God's
Covenantal relationship and support to His creation. Look how the
Old Testament names of Jehovah relate to the New Testament
ministry of Jesus, and think how often Jesus used the "I am" statement, e.g. John 6:35, 9:5, 10:11.

JEHOVAH JIREH	LORD PROVIDES	Gen. 22:14	Jesus John 1:29
JEHOVAH ROPHE	LORD HEALS	Ex. 15:26	Jesus 1 Pet. 2:24
JEHOVAH MKEDDESH	LORD SANCTIFIES	Lev. 20:8	Jesus 1 Cor. 1:30
JEHOVAH NISSI	LORD MY BANNER	Ex. 17:15	Jesus Col. 2:14–15
JEHOVAH ROHI	LORD MY SHEPHERD	Ps. 23:1	Jesus John 10:11
JEHOVAH SHALOM	LORD IS PEACE	Judg. 6:24	Jesus Rom. 5:1
JEHOVAH TSIDKENU	LORD OUR RIGHTEOUSNESS	Jer. 23:6	Jesus 2 Cor. 5:21
JEHOVAH SHAMMAH	LORD IS THERE	Ezek. 48:35	Jesus Matt. 28:20
JEHOVAH SHAPHAT	LORD OUR JUDGE	Judg. 11:27	Jesus Acts 17:31

Other names

ADONAI "MASTER" or "LORD AND MASTER". We are therefore
to be humble, obedient servants as in Nehemiah 1:11.

JEHOVAH SABAOTH LORD OF HOSTS, especially in relation
to warfare or service as in Joshua 5:14–15 and is used extensively
in the prophets, particularly Malachi.

JEHOVAH ELOHIM The SELF-EXISTENT SOVEREIGN ALL
POWERFUL STRONG ONE. This is used of God's relationship to
man as Creator and Redeemer (Gen. 2:7, 3:8) and to Israel
(Gen. 24:7).

Practical Application

We can study and meditate on these different names to understand and draw closer to an awesome, powerful but ultimately loving and merciful God. In particular we can use specific names to strengthen our faith at specific points of need. For example, when the waters roar, the mountains shake, the heathen rage and the kingdoms are moved, the psalmist comforts his heart with the assurance that "the Lord of Hosts" is with him (Ps. 46:7,11). When Hagar was rejected and all alone she found comfort in "El Roi" – "The Strong One who Sees" and who cares, encourages and strengthens. When we are hurt, He is Jehovah Rophe, when we are anxious He is Jehovah Shalom, when we need guidance He is Jehovah Rohi and when we come to an end of our own abilities He is El Shaddai. Above all, and thinking of the New Testament now, He is JEHOVAH SHUA, abbreviated to JESUS, who will "save us from our sins" and EMMANUEL, "God with us" (Matt. 1:21–23). However, perhaps in the greatest revelation of all, His Name is FATHER. HALLELUJAH!

Individual Responsibility

FORUM VOICE

It had always puzzled me why Peter and John had to be sent for to lay hands on the people of Samaria after they responded to the preaching and were baptised but did not receive the Holy Spirit. I have read various explanations, but nothing that ever really gripped me before. However, as I was re-reading the account with *Cover to Cover* I felt that the Holy Spirit was giving me new understanding.

Preaching was going on in other parts of Samaria when the believers fled from Jerusalem after the persecution following Stephen's martyrdom, but Peter and John weren't called to minister there. The explanation seems to me to be two-fold. There was Simon, the magician who professed belief and so was presumably baptised but who was not right in God's sight and not deemed fit at that time to receive the Holy Spirit (conclusion drawn from Peter's words to him). It is my belief that God did not send the Holy Spirit as He did to the household of Cornelius because of this one man. I also feel that Peter's particular gift of insight (compare the insights he was given over the Ananias and Sapphira affair) was essential in rooting out the problem and explaining it to the believers, who must have been somewhat mystified. It is a frightening thing to me that the heart of a single individual can hold up the progress of revival.

COVER TO COVER RESPONDS

We must always be careful about reading something into Scripture where Scripture itself is silent. However, your idea is certainly interesting. We know from our Old Testament studies that just one individual can either be a barrier to God's power and blessing coming upon a group of people, as in the case of Achan (Josh. 7) or the instrument of victory as in the case of David before Goliath and the whole Philistine army (1 Sam. 17). That is why each one of us is so important as an individual member of the Body of Christ and each one of us can be a barrier or a channel of His blessing and love (1 Cor. 12). Let each one of us therefore strive to be a vessel of purest gold so that Christ Himself can use us for His highest purposes (2 Tim. 2:21).

Selwyn Hughes has written an inspiring editorial on this subject in *Revival World Report* magazine published by CWR. He reflects on our tendency to often confess "our" sins and "our" coldness of heart. It was only when one young man in a prayer meeting confessed "my" sins and "my" coldness of heart that the 1949 revival came to the Hebrides, a group of islands off Scotland. Selwyn writes, "If there is to be a revival of spiritual life and power it must originate with the individual believer. We must not overlook our corporate responsibility in spiritual matters but we must not ignore our individual responsibility either. Take a few moments in your busy day to reflect on this matter. Constantly make it your prayer until it happens: 'Lord send revival, and start the work in me'."

On Reflection

- Like Ananias and Barnabas with Paul, is there someone you could encourage in the Christian faith?

- Like Peter, do you have any prejudices which need to be overcome for the gospel to flourish?

- How can you support Christians who are being persecuted today?

- Like Paul and Silas, can you use the keys of prayer and praise to unlock a difficult situation?

- Where do you fit in the Body of Christ?

- Which gifts do you currently use and which do you desire?

- How should disagreements between Christians be resolved?

- What is your own definition of love?

- Do you have any doubts about aspects of the Christian faith you could express in a loving sympathetic group?

- Have you betrayed someone in any way and failed to apologise or been betrayed and failed to forgive? How has that betrayal impacted your emotions?

CommentOn *Cover to Cover* Forum

http://www.cover2cover.org/docs/forhome.htm

12

The New Humanity "in Christ"

Ephesians has been called the "crown of all Paul's writings". It contains the cream of his theology and is a high water mark in New Testament revelation. It has been described as "the distilled essence of the Christian religion, the most authoritative and consummate compendium of our holy Christian faith".

Ephesians strikes a lyrical and majestic note. "This letter is pure music" (John Mackay). Here is "truth that sings", doctrine made melody, theology born on its knees and scored for a full orchestra of praise. It's no surprise to find the first half of the letter containing an out-pouring of worship (1:3–14), two fervent prayers (1:15–23; 3:14–19) and a doxology (3:20–21).

The Greek style adds to the effect by piling up language in long, drawn-out sentences which match the intensity of feeling being expressed. "The language of worship is dominant, the pervasive atmosphere of prayer [is] its most distinctive feature. In Ephesians, theology informs prayer and prayer itself becomes the vehicle for theology" (Luke T. Johnson).

> **Ephesians strikes a lyrical and majestic note. Here is "truth that sings", doctrine made melody.**

How did this great letter come about?

Ephesus became the scene for an extended ministry on Paul's third tour of nearly three years (Acts 19). His first act was to make good the deficiencies in understanding and experience of the 12 disciples inherited from Apollos by baptising them in water and helping them to receive the Holy Spirit (Acts 19:1–7; Eph. 1:13–14; 5:18). Later,

Paul devoted himself to a consistent teaching ministry.

Ephesus was the leading metropolis and seat of government in the Roman Province of Asia. Situated three miles from the Aegean, and connected to it by the Cayster River, the city became a rich commercial centre that "sheltered the wildest collection of pagan priests, exorcists, magicians, religious prostitutes, cultists, and charlatans in the Roman Empire" (Paul Maier).

In a story not lacking in grim humour seven sons of Sceva, who claimed to be exorcists, sought to emulate Paul in using the name of Jesus in dealing with a possessed man. Refusing to recognise their authority the man "mugged" them and left them naked and bleeding (Acts 19:13–16). The impact on the city was considerable, with fear prompting the burning of some £20,000's worth of occult books (Acts 19:19).

Notable among the city's many shrines was the great Temple of the goddess Artemis (Diana to the Romans) which was reckoned as one of the seven wonders of the world. The annual festival of Artemis in February and March, hosted thousands of pilgrims. When Paul's ministry threatened the livelihood of the idol-makers connected with the Temple, a silversmith, Demetrius, roused a riotous crowd which gathered in the magnificent 24,000-seater theatre carved into the side of the mountain overlooking the city and approached by the impressive Arcadian Way.

The church founded in such a city was set in an obviously strategic but oppressive place. It was to this church that Paul wrote his letter, perhaps around 60–61 AD, to establish the church in its new-found faith. Most contemporary NT scholars deny authorship of this letter to Paul but there is nothing in it that he could not have written. In fact the letter to the Ephesians bears striking resemblance to Paul's moving farewell address to the elders of the church there made at the nearby seaport of Miletus (Acts 20:17–38).

The purpose of the letter

Ephesians, unlike some of Paul's letters, has no distinct "problem" that needs addressing (as there is in Galatians and 1 Corinthians). For this reason, some think that Ephesians was a circular letter meant not only for Ephesus but for the other churches in the Lycus Valley (e.g. Laodicea).

What is significant is Paul's teaching on the "powers". Paul says more about the spiritual battle here than anywhere else, perhaps because Ephesus was such a well-known centre for demonic and magical practices. "This epistle is occasioned in part by Paul's special concern to address the needs of people coming to Christ from a background of what today we would call 'occult' beliefs" (Clinton Arnold).

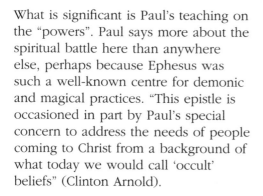

Some think that Ephesians was a circular letter meant not only for Ephesus but for the other churches in the Lycus Valley.

Paul writes to the believers to raise their awareness of the dimensions of their salvation and the high privileges of their Christian identity. Clearly, he feels they …

- need reminding of the blessings attached to being "in Christ"
- need to know God better in every way possible
- need to celebrate their distinctiveness and unique calling in the world as the new humanity created for holiness, truth, and love in the practicalities of living
- need to be energised for this task by the power of the

Spirit making Christ real within in them
- need to see themselves as soldiers engaged in battle with the cosmic powers and able to draw on the full resources of Christ's victory.

In short, Paul's aim is the formation of character, a character shaped by an abiding assurance about our Christian identity, who we are in Christ, and by an ongoing acceptance of our vocation in Christ, what our calling is. If you know who you are, you know what you're here for.

The structure of the letter
A Celebration of Christian Identity (Chapters 1–3)
Paul recalls the blessings of salvation which involve the whole Divine Trinity (1:3–14). Paul's thanksgiving leads into prayer (1:15–23), which is picked up in further prayer and doxology (3:14–21).

He recalls the way grace has transformed them out of their pagan past into their current and future enjoyment of salvation (2:1–10). Remembering their previous alienation from God's purpose he celebrates the present unity of Jew and Gentile in one body, the Church – to which Paul's ministry has so richly contributed (3:1–13).

Believers are blessed, chosen, called, loved, adopted, redeemed, forgiven and sealed by the Spirit of God – and all this is "in Christ". Everything in God's heart, everything that He is planning, all that He wills to achieve His purposes and to bring salvation to us centres in Jesus Christ. Christianity is Christ. Nothing is apart from Him. All God's fullness is in Him. "In Christ" is the key phrase. We are placed in the radical new order of reality brought about by Christ, in His death's achievement, His resurrection-life, His ascension-victory and lordly-exaltation.

To be "in Christ" is to participate in all that He is and has accomplished. We undergo a dying and a rising with Him so that we are seated with Him – within the scope and authority of His victory. To be "in Christ" is to be in a wholly new reality in history. We inhabit a whole new order of existence, a new creation. This entails a new relationship with God, a new awareness of transcendent realities – a veritable coming alive "as if from the dead", which gives us a new perspective and outlook on everything.

We need to know our "spiritual geography", to know where we are in the scheme of things; and in knowing where we are, we know who we are. We are "included by strange grace in the same love with which the Father loves the Son" (1:13), by hearing and believing the Word of truth, the gospel of salvation. This is how we become Christians.

Being "in Christ" defines who we are and where we are located on the map of reality. He is the power-field or sphere of influence in which we live and move and have our being. He is our environment. It is this which gives us an identity and a community entered into through union with Him. Often evangelicals have majored on "asking Jesus into our hearts" and "inviting Jesus into your life" – this is weak and inadequate and rarely appears in the New Testament. The New Testament speaks less of Christ being in us and more of our being in Christ.

To do otherwise is to risk domesticating grace, over-individualising salvation and trivialising God by narrowing down the scale of His plans and power. As Klyne Snodgrass puts it: "If we emphasise only that Christ is in us, we define reality and Christ is about one inch tall. If we realise we are in Christ, He determines reality and encompasses us all." This is the crucial outcome of the representative function Christ plays in the story.

Exposition of Christian Calling (chapters 4–6)

This features the theme of walking (4:1,17; 5:2,8,15). Here we can note how skilfully the opening of the letter is now re-echoed in the link between knowing more of the "hope to which he has called you" (1:18) and being urged to "live a life worthy of the calling you have received" (4:1).

Paul describes the aim of Christian living as "walking worthy of your calling". In other words to develop a way of living consistent with chapters 1–3. The image of walking as a metaphor for conduct and lifestyle is derived from the Old Testament. It corresponds to the Old Testament description of Israel's vocation as "walking in the ways of the Lord" (Deut. 10:12–13; Isa. 30:21).

> **The moral vision of the New Testament is the triumph of convictions over moods, the establishment of self-control instead of jerky uncoordinated excitement.**

"Walking in the ways of the Lord" is in other words, shorthand for Israel's ethical commission. It refutes the idea that grace immobilises us and makes us passive. On the contrary, it is grace which energises us to make choices which glorify God. Walking also suggests a course of action and decision that is considered, controlled and determined.

The moral vision of the New Testament is the triumph of convictions over moods, the establishment of self-control instead of jerky, uncoordinated excitement, of a joyful and "long obedience in the same direction". Having re-established the Ephesians in their true identity in Christ, Paul now stirs them to rise again to the challenge of their vocation as God's people. Just as Israel was called to "be holy as God is holy" and so show God's character and life on earth, so the new covenanted people of God in which Jew and Gentile join, is commissioned to take up the human vocation of being image-bearers of God in the world (4:23–24).

Chapters 4 to 6 can be understood as the challenge to express this true identity and to live out this different story as part of a new humanity. Believers, Paul argues, are called to maintain the unity of the church (4:1–6), they are called to grow towards maturity (4:7–16), to speak the truth in love (4:15). They are called to the distinctiveness of Christian living in the likeness and strength of God (4:17–5:18), in the practicalities of life (5:21–6:9).

We are called to stand firm in the spiritual battle for which Christ makes us victorious (6:10–20). Learning to do this together in the new community in radical truth and love, in forgiveness and forbearance, in giving and receiving, in home and work, is our vocation.

Empowered by the Spirit we can confront the hostile spiritual powers that seek to dehumanise and win the battle for true humanity. The vision of human formation that Ephesians sets forth presents God as our role-model (5:1). This in itself causes us to consider the limitations of psychology or the adequacy of the psychological sciences in the forming of human fullness. By definition psychology starts with the "self".

If we use psychological theories and methods alone then we leave God out of the picture. To fail to look into God's face is to become disfigured. This is a high view of humans. Yes, it takes all of God to save what He has created. This is a high calling, but Ephesians assures us that this is who we "are in Christ", redeemed and empowered by God's own Spirit for just such a vocation as the worshipping image-bearers of God in the world.

Insight

The lasting impact of the letter

In his study of the letter, Dr John Mackay, president of Princeton Seminary in the immediate post-war period, recalls his boyhood in Scotland and the impact the letter made on him. "To this book I owe my life. I was a lad of only fourteen years of age when, in the pages of the Ephesians letter, I saw a new world ... Someone had come into my soul ... I had a new outlook, new experiences, new attitudes to other people ... I had been quickened ... I was really alive."

> **Paul knows that to motivate people it is not enough to exhort them, nor even to teach them. So he reaches for their hearts.**

"In Ephesians", writes commentator, Andrew Lincoln, "Paul appeals to the deep springs of their experience, their emotions, the common values they celebrate in worship. He constantly communicates his vision of their identity through the language and forms of worship and prayer."

Paul knows that to motivate people it is not enough to exhort them, nor even to teach them. So he reaches for their hearts, to touch their emotions, to stir their imagination, to renew their adoration, to stretch their aspirations.

"People are not changed by moral exhortation but by transformed imagination" (Walter Brueggemann). And the language he uses adds to the dazzling effect, the wealth of words matching the richness of the exposition.

Paul refreshes their sense of identity, rekindles their sense of destiny and renews their hopes. He reminds them of the larger vision of what they are in Christ and fixes their goals of growth and maturity. He reinvigorates them with fresh enthusiasm, energy and confidence by directing them to Christ's abundant resources, assuring them of their ability in Him to overcome all resistance to God's will whether from sins within them or from the powers outside them.

Insight

Paul

The life of Paul has spawned whole libraries of books. It has been suggested that his influence upon the world is second only to Jesus Christ Himself. Paul's ministry to non-Jews, his missionary journeys reported in Acts and his 12 New Testament books have opened the floodgates of heaven to over one billion people throughout the earth alive today who would claim to be Christians. In this brief insight we can only scratch the surface of Paul's life, but we will look at what is probably the key of his whole life and ministry. That key is conversion.

Although the story of Paul's conversion to Christianity on the road to Damascus is dramatic enough, what is even more significant is the conversion in his whole lifestyle. Originally he was called Saul and, according to Philippians 3:4–6, he was a zealously strict Pharisee who even studied Judaism under the great rabbi Gamaliel in Jerusalem (Acts 22:3). It was his rigorous training and passionate belief in Judaism that led him to regard Christianity as a dangerous heresy that should be stamped out whatever the cost. He was a key figure in the execution of Stephen, the first Christian martyr (Acts 7:58–60).

Saul became consumed with hatred for this heresy. He "was like a wild man, going everywhere to devastate the believers, even entering private homes and dragging out men and women alike and jailing them" (Acts 8:3 TLB). Saul became aware that some believers had fled Jerusalem and so, not content with his operations there, he went to the high priest for permission to seek out these "traitors" in Damascus (Acts 9:1–3). Paul was later to refer to this part of his life in these words, "I am the worst sinner" (1 Tim. 1:15). It was on the fateful journey to Damascus that Paul had his conversion experience.

Paul's life was so dramatically converted that, according to his letter to Galatians, "That man who once persecuted us is now preaching the very message he used to try to destroy" (Gal. 1:13–23 *The Message*). Whereas Paul had previously travelled long distances to persecute disciples and destroy Christianity, he began to travel long distances to make disciples and build up Christianity. As a Pharisee he would have separated himself from Gentiles, but now he even rebuked the apostle Peter for refusing to eat with them and the student of law became the minister of grace (Gal. 2:11–21).

Saul's murderous character was so transformed that he became the apostle of love. The one who had played an important part in the stoning of Stephen and persecution of Christians was himself stoned and persecuted for the faith (2 Cor. 11:22–33). The conversion of Saul was so dramatic that even his name changed to Paul. This itself is a startling revelation of the deep transformation affected in his life. Saul means "destroyer" whilst Paul means "builder". The one who had sought to destroy Christianity became its chief builder.

We therefore see from Paul's life that no one is beyond the redemptive power of a mighty God. If even the "worst of sinners" and a vicious persecutor of the Church can be forgiven and converted, then anyone can be converted. Paul was guilty of murder, persecution, hatred, blasphemy and more besides. Yet God reached out to Paul in loving mercy to cleanse and change him. It is that conversion of Paul's character that also gives us immea-

surable hope that the same God can also take our bitter evil hearts and transform them into vast reservoirs of his love. We too, have been given a new name – Christian – "little Christ". The same powerful Spirit of Christ who empowered and transformed Paul also lives in us to reveal Jesus to others. May we, like Paul, not merely be converted in our beliefs but experience such a deep transformation in our hearts that the whole world will come to know about it!

Lydia

The story of Lydia contains important principles for our spiritual understanding. It highlights the wonderful way in which the sovereignty of God merges with the responsibility of man. The all-powerful God has committed Himself and to a certain extent limited Himself to working with frail men and women to achieve His purposes here on earth.

This is illustrated on two occasions when Jesus told the disciples where to cast their nets in order to catch fish. Both times the nets were near to breaking with record catches. Without Jesus' knowledge, the disciples would have caught no fish and, without casting their nets, Jesus' instructions would have been unfruitful. Lydia's conversion to Christianity is a perfect example of God working with us in an evangelistic setting.

Jesus always sought not just to teach His disciples academic truth but to actually involve them in the work He was doing. When He fed the five thousand, Jesus used the disciples to give the food to the crowd after blessing it, and on other occasions He actually sent them out in advance to prepare villages for His arrival. The great commission to go into all the world and preach the good news was accompanied with the promise that Jesus and His power would go with them (Matt. 28:18–20).

There are some interesting verses which open windows of understanding to this complementary partnership. Mark 16:20 records that, "the disciples went out and preached

everywhere, and the Lord worked with them and confirmed his word by the signs that accompanied it". Acts 2:47 informs us that, "the Lord added to their number daily those who were being saved". As the disciples opened their mouths and preached the good news, God touched people's hearts and they became Christians. As the disciples prayed for the sick, God touched people's bodies and they were healed. God truly "worked with them".

Lydia lived in Philippi, which was located in Macedonia. Paul had intended to preach in a number of places but God instructed him against it. Finally Paul was given a vision to go to Macedonia and arrived in Philippi. He decided to find a place of prayer where there could be people who genuinely desired to worship and know God. Paul preached the message of salvation through faith in Jesus. Just as Paul had been guided by God to that time and place, Lydia's path had also been directed to the same time and place. She was a woman who sincerely sought God and God opened her heart to respond to Paul's message (Acts 16:14).

God in His sovereignty prepared and guided both Paul and Lydia to an appointment of eternal destiny. Paul faithfully obeyed God's directions and boldly opened his mouth to preach the gospel. Lydia sought God and chose to respond to the message, repent of her sins and receive Jesus as her Saviour. Here we clearly see the beautiful way in which God works with us in order to make Himself known. His responsibility is to guide our paths, ours is to be obedient and faithfully share the gospel as He creates opportunities for us. Every new person we meet could be someone whose heart the Lord has opened to receive the good news of Jesus. Paul later wrote to the church at Corinth that God gives us seeds, we plant and water them and then God makes things grow (1 Cor. 2:3,5–9). As we pray and become sensitive to God's voice, we can become partners He works with to build a glorious Church. Hallelujah!

The Character of God

FORUM VOICE

Looking back over the readings from the last year I have to say that I sometimes found it difficult to think of the God of the Old Testament as a loving Father and as the same God who has sent His Son to die for us. In the Old Testament He seemed very vengeful and at times this has really shaken my faith.

FORUM VOICE

I think God is faithful, especially in keeping His promises to people like Abraham, Isaac, Jacob and Moses. God is holy too. I guess that's why there was destruction among the wicked Israelites. When the people turned against God, and did wicked things in His sight, I think God's holiness couldn't allow their sins to go unpunished. But in His faithfulness He sent His Son.

FORUM VOICE

I agree, to me the holiness of God our Father shines through the Old Testament. I do fear Him more now than ever before but that does not mean I love Him less. He pays so much attention to detail which makes it easy for me to believe that even the hair on our heads are numbered. Looking at the infinite freedom that Jesus accomplished on the cross for us against the heavy yoke of laws, rules and directives found in the Old Testament makes me want to leap with joy.

FORUM VOICE

What I've read in the Old Testament regarding God's character is amazing. Yes, He can be frightening, but despite all the punishment two things leap out at me. Firstly, only after His children turned away and disobeyed were they punished and secondly, God's mercy and grace will be extended to everyone if they just have faith in Him.

COVER TO COVER RESPONDS

I recently visited an aquarium and was staggered by the variety and beauty of the species of fish on display. God could have made only one grey animal, feeding on grey grass by a grey beach washed by a grey sea under a grey sky. Instead He has revealed Himself as a God of infinite variety creating breath-taking beauty. If God can do all that out of nothing then perhaps He can take my life and also turn it into something beautiful. Think too how He provided for people we have read about. He provided a wife for Adam and Isaac, a land for Abraham, Goshen for the famished clan of Jacob, manna and water for the Israelites, strength for Joshua and the sacrificial system for atonement of sin. If He can do all that perhaps He can also provide for my needs. So here are two more aspects of God's character – Beautiful Creator and Faithful Provider. Can you think of any others that build our faith and help us understand Him more? Look at the big picture and think of how you see Him through the Old and New Testament.

FORUM VOICE

God is a rock. When I am washed around by life's circumstances, my thoughts wander, my spirit drifts, my faith is weak ... God is still true and right. God is my point of reference. It is a constant surprise to me to find how solid and sure is God's truth – it is only when I realise this that I discover how far I have wandered. He has never let me down.

FORUM VOICE

Lately it occurred to me how multi-dimensional God is. What a complex and very deep personality He is – the depths of Him we will probably never know. It also occurred to me how one cannot take His Word at face value. How we need His Holy Spirit to put 3-D glasses on us to experience the depths or hidden treasures in His Word. To receive wisdom, to see life from God's point of view. God is faithful – if you ask Him to open up the Word for you – He does. Another thing that occurred to me is how God circumcises our hearts. How He takes away our hearts of stone and gives us hearts of flesh. He makes us compassionate, loving, honest, sincere, forgiving when we

235

walk in the Spirit. We become more like Him and less like the world to a point where we can feel like aliens in this world – because we are destined for Heaven! May God continue to open our eyes and ears – to experience the secret things of God.

On Reflection

- Are you in the middle of a storm and need prayer for God's comfort, peace and hope?

- Worship, prayer, hospitality, industrious, persistent, teachable, generous and caring – these are the qualities that Lydia possessed. Do you share any of them with her?

- Are you currently experiencing trials that are deepening your faith and reliance on God?

- How can you and your church fulfil the instruction to bear each other's burdens?

- How easy do you find it to avoid disputes with other Christians who are weaker in their faith?

- How can your own trials and difficulties further the gospel?

- What "works" do you think God has planned for you to do?

- Should Christians wear jewellery and expensive clothes?

- What excites you most about heaven?

- In what way is the Christian faith like warfare?

CommentOn *Cover to Cover* Forum

http://www.cover2cover.org/docs/forhome.htm

Index

PC – Windows

If you have Internet Explorer loaded on your machine

- Put CD in drive.
- Select Start Menu.
- Select Run from menu.
- type in d:\home.htm and press enter.
  (where d:\ is your CD-ROM drive.)

If you do not have Internet Explorer loaded

- Put CD in drive.
- Select Start Menu.
- Select Run from menu.
- type in d:\readme.txt and press enter.
  (where d:\ is your CD-ROM drive.)

Mac OS

If you have Internet Explorer loaded on your machine

- Put CD in drive.
- Double-click on home.htm

If you do not have Internet Explorer loaded

- Put CD in drive.
- Double-click on readme.txt

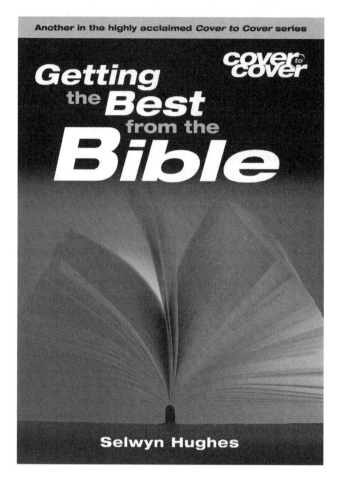

Getting the Best from the Bible

Realise the full potential of God's Word in your life. *Getting the Best from the Bible* combines inspiring devotional writing with practical guides. This essential book will teach you how to meditate on Scripture and apply biblical principles to your everyday experience. Make the time you spend reading and meditating on God's Word the most profitable hours of your life.

www.cover2cover.org

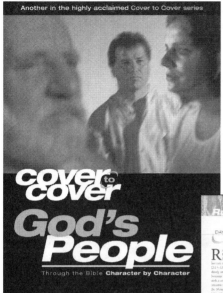

£9.95

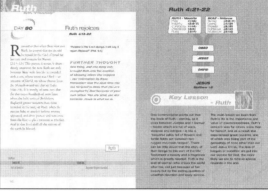

God's People

God's People is an exciting reading plan that introduces you to 58 fascinating Bible characters to reveal the amazing relationship between God and humanity. The programme is available as a softback book, a six-part collection or as a six-part subscription.

- 365 undated readings – start at any time of the year
- Selected readings taking approximately 10 to 15 minutes each day
- Key lessons on each character
- Daily comments from the authors to encourage and challenge

www.cover2cover.org

Content previously published as *Character by Character*

Cover to Cover

The chronological *Cover to Cover* programme takes you through biblical events as they happened. This invaluable tool to discovering the Bible is available as a softback and hardback book, as a six-part collection or as a six-part subscription.

- 365 undated readings – start at any time of the year
- An overview of each book
- Helpful charts, maps, diagrams and illustrations
- Daily comments from the authors to encourage and challenge

www.cover2cover.org

Content previously published as *Through the Bible Every Day in One Year*